202 Digital Photography Solutions

Solve Any Digital Camera Problem in 10 Minutes or Less

George Wallace
Chuck Gloman

McGraw-Hill

New York   Chicago   San Francisco   Lisbon
London   Madrid   Mexico City   Milan   New Delhi
San Juan   Seoul   Singapore   Sydney   Toronto

The **McGraw·Hill** Companies

Cataloging-in-Publication Data is on file with the Library of Congress

Copyright © 2003 by The McGraw-Hill Companies, Inc. All rights reserved. Printed in the United States of America. Except as permitted under the United States Copyright Act of 1976, no part of this publication may be reproduced or distributed in any form or by any means, or stored in a data base or retrieval system, without the prior written permission of the publisher.

1 2 3 4 5 6 7 8 9 0   DOC/DOC   0 9 8 7 6 5 4 3

ISBN 0-07-142168-8

The sponsoring editor for this book was Steve Chapman and the production supervisor was Sherri Souffrance. It was set in Helvetica by MacAllister Publishing Services, LLC.

Printed and bound by RR Donnelley.

 This book is printed on recycled, acid-free paper containing a minimum of 50 percent recycled de-inked fiber.

McGraw-Hill books are available at special quantity discounts to use as premiums and sales promotions, or for use in corporate training programs. For more information, please write to the Director of Special Sales, McGraw-Hill Professional, Two Penn Plaza, New York, NY 10121-2298. Or contact your local bookstore.

DEDICATION

Any endeavor one chooses that consumes hundreds of hours of time amounts to some sacrifices having to be made. If not for being anxious to race to my laptop to get my thoughts down, I would have grabbed a quick nap while our 2 year old twins were doing the same. Thanks Brooke and Connor for taking those naps of varying amounts of time. Whether I would have been taking my own quick snooze or working on this book, either way I was of little help to my wonderful wife Susan during these times; thank you Susan for your support and understanding of how important this book is to me. My mother and friends didn't see me nearly as often, but who knows, maybe they needed a break.

A special thanks goes to Jeff Dostalik, a long time friend, co-worker and owner of Absolute Imaging Digital Photography who helped dot the "I's" and cross the "T's" when I needed some reinforcement. There are others who I will personally thank and always be appreciative of and above all, they know who they are.

Without a doubt, this book would not have been possible if not for the input, guidance and tremendous support of my co-author Chuck Gloman. Chuck gave me the encouragement, support and expertise that I lacked in creating what we feel is an informational and hopefully somewhat lighthearted introduction to the world of digital photography. Thanks Chuck, you're the best!

Contents

Preface

We were initially hoping for 999 or 1,003 solutions, but we all have our limitations. As a reader or when reviewing a book, we must determine when enough is enough. At first, we thought we had 202 solutions in the past year alone, when in fact we actually had 202 experiences or situations. Hopefully, as you review and read this book, you'll find the answer to a question that you've personally had or encountered.

We've always considered ourselves to have been on the front line of the evolution from conventional photography (shooting film) to the ever popular world of digital photography. We feel we've been extremely fortunate as we've had the opportunity to shoot black and white 35mm and medium-format film, hand-processed the negatives in stainless steel containers, developed prints in a tray, and watched the image appear in an almost magical manner. The same process happens in digital photography, only you see the results immediately without sticking your hands in chemicals (unless you want to). Nobody needs to shoot with a digital camera to find photography a unique and rewarding experience, but it's the endless possibilities when shooting digital that make it so intriguing.

The title of this book, *202 Digital Photography Solutions*, is accurate in that 202 different solutions exist for problems you might encounter when shooting digital images. Ranging from a few sentences to several pages in length, each solution was gleaned from our experiences.

As you will notice, a number of similarities exist between 35mm film and digital photography. This new medium really has no drawbacks and you now have the luxury of immediately seeing the results of your labors on a *liquid crystal display* (LCD) screen.

We also bring the digital filmmaking side to the equation because our motion picture and video experience began in 1977. However, our photography experience began when we were first able to hold and point a Kodak Instamatic 134 camera at our intended target, and we have been taking photographs ever since.

Throughout this text we use the term "we" because this book is a collaborative effort. Since we both are speaking as one person (it's hard to do) rather than saying "I did this or that," we both have experienced everything in this book firsthand, and we hope to impart some of that wisdom (or lack thereof) onto you, our readers.

We also hope you will pick up this book and use it as a reference when you encounter difficulties on a photo shoot. The best way of learning is by doing, and once you have a camera, you should take advantage of the information presented in this book. Never be afraid to tackle any significant project because it is "beyond your capabilities." Just because you haven't done something before does not mean you cannot do something new. If you try and fail, simply try again . . . and again until you succeed.

We promise that digital photography is a very rewarding field (not necessarily monetarily). If you have the desire to learn and just want to go out and shoot pictures, don't let anyone stop you or tell you otherwise. Just do it and you might be writing the sequel to this book.

George Wallace
Chuck Gloman

Chapter 1

Beginnings

#1 Where to Start

This book was written to help you better understand and use your digital camera. Throughout Chapter 1, we will discuss the basics. Whether you are new to the field of digital photography or an established professional, this chapter will help you learn what's out there.

The first chapter explains where to start, what a digital camera really is, how to choose the right camera, how to best determine a camera's capabilities, and the differences between digital and 35mm cameras. It also covers how to get the most out of point and shoot cameras, deciding how many megapixels you really need, and determining if resolution is important. The chapter will also look at how to use a high-end camera, deciding if you need interchangeable lenses, and how to take your first digital picture.

#2 What Is a Digital Camera?

With all the different types of cameras available, what does a digital camera do that is different from the myriad of other disposal cameras on the market?

A digital camera uses electronics rather than film to capture its image. A film camera opens its iris, allowing the incoming light to expose the negative film. A digital camera allows light to enter the camera the same way, but instead of exposing film, it is captured by a *charge-coupled device* (CCD). This CCD then sends the image to a storage medium. Not to oversimplify anything, but that's basically what a digital camera does. Both function the same way, but a digital unit will store the picture electronically on something other than film.

Throughout the rest of the solutions in this book, we will discuss how to best use your digital camera to capture images you'll be proud to share with others — without the expense of purchasing film, waiting to have it processed, and paying even more to print the results so you can see them.

Just like the TV commercials in 1965 announced, "Welcome to the Radial Age" (the steel-belted radial tire was introduced), today in the twenty-first century, "Welcome to the Digital Age."

#3 How to Choose the Right Camera

Now that digital photograph is here to stay and more readily affordable, how do you choose the camera that's best for your needs?

The first questions you need to ask are, what is your main purpose for purchasing a digital camera and what do you primarily want to shoot? If your goal is to have any family member be able to pick up the camera and grab that "special shot" quickly, keep it simple. You don't need a camera with a lot of bells and whistles if you just want to get a good digital image at an affordable price.

Are your needs more professional? Should the camera accept different lenses, offer a variety of image sizes or storage devices, or match an existing 35mm camera? Do you want a camera that travels with you? A lower-end camera can fit easily in a briefcase, purse, or your car's glove compartment. Features like auto-focus, auto-exposure, and a fixed lens will keep the camera compact, but the real item that miniaturizes any camera is the number of megapixels.

Some people want a camera that will fit in their pockets, but they still want the quality that a 4-megapixel camera offers. A few cameras like this are available, but for $200 or less, even smaller 1- or 2-megapixel digital cameras will also do the trick.

No one, not even the friendly authors of this book, can tell you which camera will best suit your needs. Do your research and homework. Look at cameras in stores. How do they feel in your hand (the cameras, not the stores)? Are the features too complicated or too small to operate easily? Because you are the one that will use this device, you should see if it's possible to take or shoot several images (test photos), whether in the store or elsewhere. That is the only way to see if it fits your needs.

When purchasing a new camera, we always try to rent or borrow it for a weekend shoot to see if we like it. Sometimes you discover that it's not what you expected; other times, it's perfect. If it isn't a marriage made in heaven, at least with this approach you didn't spend a fortune.

Don't buy a particular camera because someone else likes it. In case you haven't noticed, everyone is different. Everyone also has their preferences on which equipment they use, and many people stick with what works for them. Nikon people won't even look at Canons and vice versa. (Kodak, however, makes cameras that accept Nikon and Canon mount lenses; so does Fuji and so on.) Base your decision on what you want the camera to do. You're the one that has to live with it.

#4 How to Determine a Camera's Capabilities

When you're holding that shiny new digital camera in your hands, the first thing you should do is see what it is capable of doing. Are the pictures sharp, can you adjust settings, will it hold up to your needs, or will you outgrow it soon? You should have a good idea of what you want. Now you need to see if the camera will do it.

You should never be in a hurry to make a digital camera purchase. These aren't disposable, one-time-use cameras. Instead, they are sophisticated, electronic marvels that will do amazing things. Plenty of good digital camera manufacturers are out there and they all want to help you make a decision—to buy their camera.

Do your research on the Internet, and then go to your local camera or large discount store. We recommend your local camera store, as they deal strictly with cameras (maybe camcorders and accessories also), and are normally more knowledgeable about cameras in general than someone at a large discount store. More importantly, you can actually see and hold the camera. That's hard to do from a mail-order house.

Prices will also be cheaper at a mail-order house because they deal in bulk. A local shop will stand behind their camera (because they are behind the counter where the cameras live) and a little more money will give you access to the sales people again if you should have problems.

Ask if they have literature on the camera you're interested in or, better yet, see if they have a copy of the user's manual that you can browse through. Don't be rushed by someone looking at his watch and constantly asking if you are ready to make a decision. Check what the manual has to say about the camera's capabilities. If you find something close to what you want but that may be missing a couple features, ask the salesperson if he or she has any recommendations. Revisit the Internet if necessary after shopping around. Really good deals are offered all the time and can be ordered directly online. Sometimes Internet dealers throw in additional accessories if they really want to make the camera more attractive to the buyer.

Like buying a car, few people walk right in and purchase one. A digital camera, although costing less, should be no different. You need to see it, drive it, look at all the options, and come back later when you've checked out the competition. You may find some great deals because the store is overstocked or discontinuing an item. Check to see if the display camera is available at a reduced price.

You may have visited local stores, seen the cameras, and found the same things offered on the Internet for much less. What do you do? The same warranty was offered, no state tax had to be paid, and the shipping cost was less than $10. We would never do this with a camera, sight unseen. Some digital cameras have been offered for less than $50 on the Internet. When they arrive, they are less than 1 megapixel and can store about 2 images. The old adage is you get what you pay for.

Learn the terminology and see what the camera does. If one model doesn't suit you, maybe the next step up will be better, or try another manufacturer. Kmart and Wal-Mart have tons of digital cameras on little leashes in their photo department. Thousands have held them and tried them out, but that's the only way to make an educated decision.

If you purchase a camera with less than you really wanted, it will remain unused and you've wasted your money. But by knowing the camera's capabilities — it wouldn't sit around for long — you'll be using it.

#5   Which Is Better: 35mm or Digital?

There are three things you should never talk about: religion, politics, and which is better, film or digital. Most people think this is a difficult question, but it really isn't. You, the user, must decide which is best for you.

Both formats are great at what they do and you should weigh the decision carefully. Digital is extremely fast, is easy to use, and does not have to be an expensive purchase. With digital, you have no film to load, accidentally expose, or jam. You can shoot and immediately view the images without having the negative processed and printed, only to find out Aunt Wilma had her eyes closed the whole time. You now can make sure you have the picture you want, even if it's not Aunt Wilma.

If that weren't enough, you can take that image (the one with her eyes open) and within minutes send it via e-mail to anyone you want (even those you don't). You can also create digital greeting cards, which could also be done from a color print shot on 35mm by personally scanning it or having a local lab do it for you.

Many people feel that the quality of the prints is much better if shot on film with a 35mm camera. In many cases, this may be true due to the fact that some digital users may not be using a quality printer, good photographic paper, or have a camera without enough megapixels. 35mm has been around for a long time and delivers pristine images.

The other issue we hear is that, "I already have a good 35mm camera that I spent a lot of money on with all the different lenses and filters. Do I really need both?" Once again, this is an answer only you can make. We still have great manual-focus cameras that take incredible pictures. When auto-focus came along, we had tons of lenses that were no longer necessary. Also, as we get older, the camera can focus faster and sharper than our tired eyes.

True, you never need to buy film or have it processed and printed, only to find you ran out before you finished shooting. But what happens when you just took the most amazing shot of your life and you still have 35 images left to shoot on the roll? How do you know the first or last image on the roll will turn out? These are problems with 35mm that digital does not have.

At the same time, you need to be sure to download or delete images from your digital camera periodically to allow you to continue shooting. One thing you can count on is that the overall ease and quality of the digital process will continue to make great strides.

The final decision may be that if you already have a good 35mm camera, use it when it makes sense (such as making oversize prints to be mounted and framed). But when you want to have images available at once, get out the digital camera. If you think this is a difficult decision, which is better: a large comfortable sedan that is safe; an SUV that provides lots of room inside, has four-wheel drive, can flip over at high speeds, and is a gas guzzler; or a small compact car that gets 50 miles per gallon, that's easy to park, but that scares you to death when the next tractor trailer is about to pass. If you make the right decision, let us know.

#6 How to Get the Most out of Point and Shoot Cameras

The point and shoot camera is the easiest digital camera to use. As the name implies, you point it at the subject and you immediately have a digital image. The more you use it, the better you will become.

The lowest-priced digital cameras available are the point and shoot models, where you frame your subject in the viewfinder and take a shot by pressing the shutter release button. The cameras may be reflex (where you see exactly what the lens sees) or nonreflex when the image in the viewfinder is a close approximation of what the lens will see.

These cameras have very few options and not many features. For instance, if your camera comes equipped with a 3X optical zoom, you may find that this is not quite enough to get you close. You'll either need to take what you can and enlarge your image size later or try to get closer to your subject to fill up the frame.

On the opposite end, you may also be limited with your wide-angle capabilities with a point and shoot. Try to get back as far as possible to include everything you want in your final image.

These cameras are light and compact, and they are designed to do a really nice job at an affordable price. Sometimes this is all you need to document something. We know people who use these to get a digital inventory of their possessions, real estate agents who can immediately get an image of a home to post on the multilisting, dentists who build crowns from a quick digital snapshot, and insurance adjustors who need an instantaneous image of the claim.

Whatever the purpose, a point and shoot camera is the fastest way to digitally capture an image and view the results. The point and shoot is also a great way to experiment with the digital photography world around us.

#7 How Many Megapixels Do I Need?

When working in digital photography, the term megapixel will keep cropping up. The word is used to define how powerful the camera really is. The greater the number of megapixels, the sharper and more defined the image. But how many megapixels do you really need?

First, let's define what a megapixel is. This isn't *Webster's* definition; it's ours (the words we will use are smaller). A pixel is one tiny point or dot on a CCD that your camera uses to collect an image. Digital video cameras and still cameras have these CCDs. The term mega means million. So a megapixel means a camera that has 1 million pixels, which is quite a lot.

When you shop for digital cameras, all manufacturers give a pixel description in megapixels for the camera's capabilities. You can get cameras at 1.2 megapixels, 2.1, 3.5, 4.3, and so on. Most aren't an even number like 2 or 4 million pixels; instead they will be listed with a decimal point, which indicates another hundred thousand or so pixels. A 3.3 megapixel camera isn't as sharp as a 3.5, which offers another 200,000 pixels.

Let's go back and answer the previous question: How many megapixels do you need? Well, it depends on what you want to do with your images and how much you want to spend. Like buying grapefruit, the more you purchase, the higher the bill.

A point and shoot 1-megapixel camera will cost very little and still deliver an image with 1 million pixels. But the resolution of the image will be grainy or pixely at best. These cameras are best if you want to take a shot and then e-mail it to someone. The picture, because of its size and resolution, will take very little time to upload and download. People with phone modems will appreciate not spending a week trying to download an image of Junior taking his first bite of pizza.

Two megapixel cameras are a little more mainstream and will capture better images. You can still e-mail the results, but it will take a bit longer to download unless you compress the size of the file. Two megapixel cameras are great for 4×6 images, which is the print size most people use for their 35mm cameras. The pictures are sharp and you will have paid a little more for the digital camera.

The largest variety resides in the 3-megapixel range with 3.1 and 3.2 being the most popular. This size of CCD can reproduce a strikingly sharp image up to 8×10. If it is any larger, you are going see flaws, but few people even reproduce an image larger than 8×10 (frames are harder to find above that size) and that's why these cameras are so popular among the masses.

The 4-megapixel range is where the pros begin to dwell. The cameras start costing over $500 and your images look great at 11×14 and 16×20. Obviously, these are large pictures! Of course, you can always reprint smaller images that will be sharp, but if you want something very big and friendly, 4 megapixels will get you there in style.

The 5- and 6-megapixel family is definitely at the professional level with the Fuji cameras, the Nikons, and the Canons all living here. At the time of writing, these are the largest megapixel cameras readily available to the public, such as the Nikon D100 at 6.1 megapixels. Canon is offering a 14-megapixel camera soon, but we haven't seen or held it yet. A camera this sharp we will use quite a lot!

Using Table 1-1, you can determine which number of megapixels will fulfill your needs. Just keep in mind that the cameras will get better with time (more megapixels) and cost less. But that's just the industry.

TABLE 1-1 Megapixels and What They Will Do

Number of Megapixels	Largest Image Reproduction
1 megapixel	E-mail images
2 megapixels	4 × 6
3 megapixels	8 × 10
4 megapixels	16 × 20
5 megapixels	As large as you'd like
6 megapixels	Seen from a small aircraft

#8 Is Resolution Important?

Once again, this is a question that you need to be able to answer. Resolution is how sharp a digital image appears to be. The greater the number of *dots per inch* (dpi), the sharper or clearer the image. The downside is the higher the dpi, the larger your file size, and usually the longer it takes to print or send.

It's important to take your digital picture with the greatest resolution possible. Granted, this will take up more space on your storage medium, but it is easier to reduce the resolution later for printing or storage purposes than to try to add resolution after the fact. Adding resolution is possible, but the image never looks the same and appears to be enhanced (because it is).

Resolution is important and you may want to consider the following with regards to the type of job you're doing and the ideal resolution. Table 1-2 lists various dpi ratings.

Knowing the end use of your digital images helps you determine the correct dpi in which to shoot. We've sent images for publication that were 600 dpi and the images in this book were to be 1200 dpi. When using Photoshop or other software applications, you can change the dpi resolution. Still it's better to shoot higher and reduce for printing or storage.

Printers have fast draft printing settings that are usually 300 dpi. The image is viewable, but not extremely sharp. In order to quickly view and print an image on photographic paper, 300 dpi will save you time and ink.

The normal setting on most inkjet printers is 600 dpi, much sharper than the fast mode and slower in printing. The best quality, or the

TABLE 1-2   Dpi Ratings

Black and white newsletters and flyers	180 dpi
Black and white images for laser printing	120 dpi
Color images for laser printing	180 dpi
Color images for web pages	72 dpi
Color inkjet printers	300 dpi
Color images for magazines or similar publications	300 dpi & up

"photo" setting, on most printers is the 1200 dpi mode. Printers can take over 5 minutes to produce a color 8×10 image at this resolution.

What happens if you shoot or store an image at 300 dpi and print it out at 1200 dpi? The image will never look better than its original setting and any flaws will be enlarged. What about shooting or saving at 1200 dpi and printing at 300 dpi? The images will actually look better because the original was saved at a higher format and printed out in a draft mode to save time and ink. This is the preferred method with professionals. With images at 2400 dpi and above, laser printers are the only way to get accurate and true reproductions at those resolutions.

#9 How to Use a High-End Camera

Someone might want to purchase a high-end camera for a lot of reasons. Some think it may make them look more professional to show off a brand-name camera (such as Fisher-Price), while others just want to take better, sharper images.

If you choose to go with a high-end digital camera, you're either a serious hobbyist, have aspirations of becoming a professional photographer, or you are already a professional. The other scenario may be that you have more money than you know what to do with. If that is the case, we'll send you an address to help our favorite charity (not us, a real charity—not a charity case).

If you're willing to spend a fair amount of money, you can purchase a high-end digital camera that is compatible with conventional photography equipment, especially from manufactures such as Nikon and Canon. Kodak, Fuji, and others sell digital cameras that use Canon and Nikon lenses.

Since you'll probably be able to use your existing lenses, flash units, and filters interchangeably, which will negate additional accessory purchases, a higher-end camera will take you from the 35mm world into the digital one.

For the medium-format cameras, such as Hasselblad, Bronica, or Mamiya, digital backs can be purchased that enable you to use the same camera body and lenses you'd use for your pictures. These cameras take phenomenal images in their film format, but by using a digital back, you access the same crystal-clear optics without the hassle of film. A digital back is a capture device that allows a film camera to record digital images — much like a lesser quality Polaroid back that could also be used.

Many professional studio photographers have decided to use digital backs on their 4×5 view cameras as opposed to shooting film, but again this is a major investment and their customers need to buy into the digital idea. The capabilities and operation of the digital backs vary from one manufacturer to another, so research is the key as far as which direction the serious photographer should take.

Digital is clearly an option for professionals with medium-format cameras for the same reasons others use digital cameras: immediate results, image manipulation, and large storage capacity.

Numerous wedding photographers have switched to digital cameras because the initial outlay of cash for film stock and processing (usually over a $1000) is negated with a digital camera. The digital photographer can see if the bride's eyes were closed immediately, and the look of that special effects filter can be determined right away.

Whatever the reason for your desire to purchase a high-end camera, do your research and see which model and manufacturer has the features you want. If this doesn't suit you, use a piece of masking tape and write an expensive name across the front of your camera like Rolex, Rolls Royce, or Cadillac. None of these people make cameras, but you will feel expensive.

#10 Do I Need Interchangeable Lenses?

An interchangeable lens adds a little more weight to your camera package. Most cameras come with a lens that covers wide-angle to normal to telephoto all in one. Why would you possibly need more lenses?

The answer to this question depends upon the type of pictures you intend to take and how much flexibility and creativity you want to have when shooting. With a basic, lower-end digital camera, you'll have a button or control that will contain a W (for wide angle) and a T (for telephoto). If that area of coverage variation is all you need to take the pictures you want, then you don't need interchangeable lenses. You may not need to use additional lenses for different photo opportunities if you are satisfied with the limitations of the fixed lens on the camera.

What you need to consider is if the "W" is actually going to give you a wide enough angle of view. Will you be able to capture the crowd shots, landscapes, sporting events, candids of the children playing, and other pictures that cover a large area? Wanting just a little bit more won't help if you can't switch lenses.

Sometimes a wider lens is best if you shoot a lot of large groups or landscape shots. Possibly 5 millimeters wider is all you need. Times will occur when a 28mm lens, although wide, isn't wide enough.

The same would hold true for the "T." Your fixed lens with its telephoto at its fullest may not allow you to capture an object that is far off in the distance. If you get too close to the panther, you may be its lunch. A longer lens will still keep you at a safe distance but allow you to get up close and personal. You may be forced to take the picture at the camera's maximum telephoto setting and later you'll need to point out to someone that the little speck in the middle of the image is a rare bald eagle from Pennsylvania.

If you spend most of your time shooting sporting events from the sidelines, a long telephoto will get you much closer to the action. Little Junior or Juniorette playing in his or her first big game may be impossible to see without a long lens. You'll want to see their faces, not just their bodies, in an extremely long shot. Figure 1-1 illustrates the longest

Figure 1-1

The image was shot at 135mm with a point and shoot camera.

Figure 1-2

This image was shot at 210mm. Which is best?

telephoto position on a point and shoot camera with a fixed focus. Figure 1-2 shows the results of using an interchangeable lens with a more powerful magnification.

A good friend of ours has a well-known brand-name camera with image capture capabilities ranging from 38mm to 115mm, which is standard for that particular camera, and a 3x optical zoom. He is completely pleased with the wide-angle and telephoto options available.

Many of us, however, would prefer to have a 28mm or, for certain occasions, even a 20mm lens on the camera so we can capture the best possible picture. Also, a 115mm telephoto falls far short of many people's idea of a telephoto lens. Some feel they need at least a 250mm lens to even come close to filling the frame with the object. The need for interchangeable lenses is not unlike trying to determine if you need four-wheel drive in your vehicle. Some do; some don't. It's entirely up to you.

#11 How to Take Your First Picture

Getting your first digital camera is thrilling. You can now do things that weren't possible with your 35mm. But before you begin, a few things will help you ease into the transition to digital.

Don't be in a big hurry to take that first award-winning digital picture. When purchasing a camera, carefully examine the exterior of the box and make sure no signs of any visible damage exist. Overzealous shippers may have played a quick game of touch football with your prized possession.

After unpacking your digital camera, make sure that everything has been supplied and that no cables or vital pieces are missing. Take a few minutes and do some basic maintenance. As with every toy or piece of equipment we purchase, a user's manual is included. Take the time to *read through the entire manual* with the camera nearby, so you can relate to what is being discussed in each section.

Review the table of contents and the index to see if you don't understand something or need to do some further research. Each digital camera will vary slightly, but certain tasks should be performed before you begin to shoot. You'll have within your setup mode a series of menus that allow you to set up the camera for the correct language, time, date, and other features that may include setting up the picture-taking modes.

Check the lens of the camera to be sure it has no scratches. Before taking your first picture, make sure the surface of the lens is clean. Special lens-cleaning fluid and lint-free tissues should be used, but sparingly.

At this point, you're probably feeling pretty confident that this is going to be fun (and maybe a little challenging), but you're ready. Experiment with the camera by shooting anything and everything under several different conditions. In other words, "get the bugs out" before an opportunity exists to take a meaningful picture. Shoot and review many times. After all, you're not wasting film, spending money on processing, or waiting and paying for meaningless pictures. You know immediately what you've done and, if necessary, how you can improve your images.

Chapter 2

Digital Cameras

#12 What Digital Cameras Are All About

Now that you're learning more about digital cameras, it may be time to begin the purchasing process. That includes purchasing a digital camera that's right for you, how to set the time and date on a camera, how to best use the *liquid crystal display* (LCD) window and viewfinder, the things every digital camera should have, which options make life easier, and how to use an inexpensive point and shoot camera.

#13 How to Purchase a Digital Camera That's Right for You

Just like cameras, every person is different and has different wants and needs, as well as strengths and weaknesses. You need to ask the right questions to determine which camera is the best one for you.

The first thing you're going to hear when you tell someone that you're going to buy a digital camera is advice, and sometimes too much of it. Your neighbor is going to tell you that she and her husband have a camera that's compact, inexpensive, and really easy to use, and it's the one you should get (it also floats in the bathtub).

Your best friend is going to tell you about the great deal he got on his digital camera and there's nothing comparable on the market, if you don't mind your camera falling off the back of a truck. Neither of these people is necessarily right or wrong, it's just what they believe. Everyone has opinions; that's why they're free, but these opinions may be useful to help you weed out what you don't want.

Ask your friends, colleagues, and neighbors what they like best about the cameras, and least. What was their reason for getting a camera and are they the same as your needs? The bottom line is, what are you going to use your camera for the majority of the time?

If you're going to be photographing your son playing football and, as a parent, your only opportunity to shoot is from Section F, Row 6, close to low-flying aircraft, you're going to need a digital camera with interchangeable lenses. Shooting from that distance, you're going to need at least a 500mm lens or Mount Palmer's telescope to get a decent picture.

A friend of ours purchased a digital camera just to shoot his son playing basketball. Unfortunately, he will not be allowed on the court and the images he will get with 1.2 megapixels from a different time zone aren't going to be much use. Like the previous example, he really needs a camera with interchangeable lenses, something that can get closer to the subject from his vantage point. Figure 2-1 shows an image from his camera and Figure 2-2 displays a shot from a camera with a 400mm lens.

When you're not at the stadium or basketball court, let's say you're going to photograph some of your rare coins and put them on eBay. That's when you'll need a close-up lens or a bellows extension on your camera to show that your coin is in mint condition and is priced accordingly. That little point and shoot won't suffice.

If, by chance, your only intention is to photograph the kids and send out e-mail with pictures attached, you can buy a lower-end, less expen-

Figure 2-1

Playing basketball as seen
through a point and shoot
1.2 megapixel camera

Figure 2-2

Using a longer lens, a better shot of the action is achieved.

sive camera that would be ideal to get those images out to friends and relatives. Or if you want to photograph the first steps your child takes, you will be close to the action (unless he or she takes their first steps in a stadium). I guess you know you're a sports addict if that happens.

The camera manufacturers understand that the buyer has different needs and requirements, which is why you have so many digital cameras from which to choose. Input from others is great, but purchase the camera that's going to be the best for what you want to do. You know your specific circumstances better than anyone else. This is a decision only you should make.

#14 How to Set the Time and Date on a Digital Camera

When you first get your digital camera, the battery that allows you to adjust the time and date is probably not inserted. The battery would otherwise languish and drain if it resided in the camera.

Once home with your purchase, inserting the battery should be one of the first things you do to help you get better acquainted with your digital camera. Battery insertion information is normally located in the beginning of your digital camera's user guide. If not, look in the index and find where that section is located.

The first thing you need to do after inserting the battery is turn the camera on and press the Menu button. The batteries that power the camera are not the same ones that remember things like the time and date; that is a cell or button battery that remains in the camera at all times. The other batteries should be removed if the camera won't be used for extended periods of time.

Each camera is slightly different, but on the Menu page (as seen on your LCD screen) you should see a Setup Menu Page or something similar. You'll probably have choices on the menu such as Brightness, Auto Transfer, Sequence Number, Date, and Auto Off. You'll want to locate and highlight the Date Menu. This gives you access to those features. From the Date Menu, you can highlight Year, Month, and Day, and choose the order in which they're displayed. The choice is yours; just be sure you set it correctly. Once set, it will automatically change until the battery dies or is removed.

Setting the time is usually done right after the date is set. Your choices are standard or military time (numbers above 12 displayed as 13, 14, and so on). If you choose standard, set the AM or PM feature to avoid confusion later on.

If requested, be sure to save the changes in the settings so you'll only have to go through this exercise once. This information will be displayed on each image you take in the future or it may be switched off. Even if you never intend to display the time and date on your images, set this feature so you have access to it if you ever change your mind, not that that would ever happen.

#15 How to Use the LCD Window and Viewfinder

One of the first things people must get used to is having an LCD on the camera. In the days of film photography, the operator peered through a viewfinder and snapped the picture. You still do that with a digital camera, but having an LCD screen allows you to immediately review the shot before saving it for posterity. The newer digital cameras generally have both an optical viewfinder (the one you look through) and an LCD display screen (the one you look at) on the back of the camera for composition and picture review.

The brightness and size of the LCD varies with different models, with some barely visible in daylight. Try to get a model with a bright screen and one with shading provided by the camera for easier viewing. Check or ask to see if the LCD operates in cold weather because some do not.

LCD screens are not available in many different sizes, with most being about two inches in diameter. A larger LCD screen is easier to view than a smaller one, especially if the larger display is brighter, but the camera will cost more and the screen will pull more power. No sure way exists for determining how much power the LCD screen consumes, but rest assured it is a major drain on the camera's battery.

If you are shooting pictures in rapid succession and want to review the results later, there is no sense in having the LCD screen illuminated. It just drains the batteries and helps light up your face for others to see. Simply turn it off. On the other hand, if you want to review each image after you shoot it, that's what the screen was designed for.

You cannot frame the image on the LCD screen when shooting unless it's a video camera. Likewise, the optical viewfinder will not display the image you recently captured. You won't get these two mixed up, and in very little time you'll never believe how you got along without them.

#**16** What Every Digital Camera Should Have

When purchasing a digital camera, a few must-haves will allow you to capture the best images possible. The following list of terms isn't in any specific order, but each is important in making up the entire package.

The list includes an optical zoom lens, a hot shoe for an external flash, a tripod socket, a slot for removable media, an LCD screen and status report, an optical viewfinder that lets you see and frame the shot before capturing it, and a handgrip molded to the camera body, which is imperative if you want your camera to hold up to the abuses of everyday use. One that isn't molded to the body will break quickly under stress (just like we do).

An eyelet or loop for a neck strap will help you find the camera when you misplace it because it's hanging around your neck. This feature also helps prevent theft because someone would rather steal something in your pocket or purse but not hanging around your neck. Besides it helps you look the tourist part.

A built-in electronic flash will give you more light when needed, outdoors or inside. This supplemental light is sometimes what's needed to get that special shot or to fill in existing shadows. A user's guide is also necessary, because no matter how well trained or experienced you may be, the user's guide is your bible and blueprint for understanding how your camera functions. Carry this with you at all times and you will never be at a loss when taking a digital photo.

#17 How to Use an Optical Zoom Lens

This is a feature that allows you to zoom from wide angle to telephoto while you stay stationary. Being the sharpest and most expensive type of zoom, it is more accurate and less pixely than its counterpart, the digital zoom. The digital zoom takes the optical image and electronically enhances it by enlarging the grain. This degrades the image on anything larger than 3X.

#18 How to Use a Hot Shoe for an External Flash

One of our favorite features is the hot shoe. A hot shoe is a metal bracket on the top of your camera that accepts an external flash. The camera may come with a built-in flash, but rarely is this enough illumination for most users. Having a hot shoe allows you to attach another flash to the top of the camera, reducing red eye and providing a larger amount of light.

#19 How to Use the Slot for Removable Media

Every camera should have a storage port that contains the memory module. All but the cheapest cameras let you remove the card when it's full or insert one with a larger capacity. Cameras without this feature will have memories that quickly fill up with data (just like your favorite aunt). A removable card lets you keep taking images indefinitely.

#20 How to Read an LCD Status Report

This is something that will tell you the parameters of the image you recently captured, with information on the f-stop, shutter speed, exposure, and so on. The report lets you determine if you need to adjust any of the specific details of the image. Using a menu-type feature, you can scroll through and call up information on the LCD screen. This is your means for learning what is happening within the camera.

#21 How to Use a Tripod Socket

A tripod socket lets you mount the camera on something steadier than your picket fence or palm. Longer exposure times require a steady, immovable camera. If you want to get into the shot, having a tripod beats throwing the camera in the air hoping it snaps and frames the picture correctly on the way down.

#22 How to Use the Menu

A menu selection for shooting in various conditions will be displayed on your LCD screen. Although no two conditions for shooting are ever the same, a digital camera that allows you to control your destiny will improve your chances of getting the picture. If you ever shoot in bright, direct sunlight, you will need controls like this. You may encounter shooting conditions affected by clouds or darkness, or the shot may be backlit, have a preferred aperture, be a portrait, or be a macro (extremely close).

#23 Which Options Make Life Easier?

The items listed in this solution are not vital to taking better images, but they certainly do help. The items listed in the previous solution you must have; these just make your life a little better.

Some features are options on a given model, such as red-eye reduction, a low battery warning, automatic flash, cable release (if applicable), a self-timer, auto-focus, a time exposure setting, and a macro close-up, but they may be standard on other models. The more expensive the digital camera, the more features will be standard.

The self-timer is especially useful when you're taking a picture of a group of family or friends and you're expected to be in the picture (or want to be). The self-timer will allow you to hurriedly join the group after hitting the shutter release button. As mentioned last time, without a tripod socket, this is next to impossible. But if a self-timer is offered, the tripod acceptance will also be featured.

When someone looks at the picture and asks who framed it so perfectly, you can be quite the hero and say you were actually in the picture you composed. At least be humble about it.

The manufacturers of digital cameras have so many options with their different models that it can be mind-boggling. Visit your friends, the Internet, and local shops to get an idea of the options available from a variety of cameras and try to decide which will best suit your needs.

If you know of an option you think you might be able to use someday or would make your picture taking more enjoyable, check if that option is affordable. External accessories like extra storage capability, card readers, and attachments aren't really considered options, but if they are available with the camera, ask and see if it's something you could use.

#24 How to Use Point and Shoot Cameras

How many times and in how many ways have we heard the expression point and shoot? We're not talking about guns, of course, but digital cameras. These are usually small, inexpensive cameras that are used as the name implies. The lens is fixed (noninterchangeable), focusing is unnecessary, everything is automatic with very few manual settings, and a built-in flash helps out in dark situations.

These cameras are usually for beginners or people who may want images in a hurry without the bother of a more elaborate digital camera. The megapixel range may be from 1.2 to 5, mostly depending on the price.

Let's think about point and shoot from a digital camera perspective. When considering the purchase of a digital camera, ask yourself if the actual size of the camera is important. Do you want to be able to have the camera fit in your pocket or do you plan on storing it in a small camera bag or purse? The smaller and more portable cameras will have a small LCD screen and also contain smaller storage devices (memory cards or chips).

A camera with a digital zoom lens as opposed to an optical zoom also tends to be smaller because of the circuitry involved. If the digital camera is your first experience shooting digital or if a child may be using the camera, consider purchasing something on the lower end of the scale. If you don't want to spend a lot of time and effort thinking about the perfect image and cost is still a factor, start with a point and shoot model.

With these cameras, you'll find you have few options, but if you simply want to take a quick shot digitally, this is probably the camera for you. Remember, you won't have high-resolution or low-light capabilities, a large storage device, a zoom lens, or many other options available with the more expensive cameras. Shooting in low light conditions may also be difficult.

Obviously, you won't be able to be very creative with a point and shoot camera, but they can take a nice overall digital picture. These cameras can be very practical on horseback rides, at concerts, amusement parks, swimming pools, and other events where you merely want to record the activities as they happen with little bother or inconvenience. Many people consider the point and shoot digital camera as being comparable to a conventional single-use camera, with the exception that you *can* use it more than once without the expense or hassle of film and processing.

Chapter 3

Lenses

#25 What Lenses Can Do for You

A lens is the camera's eye to the world and is the most important element a camera can have. In this chapter, we will discuss how to pick the best lens from the wide selection available; how to care for and maintain lenses; how to use wide-angle, normal, portrait, and telephoto lenses; how to use a doubler or converter; and how 35mm and digital lenses differ.

#26 How to Pick the Best Lens

As we've stated many times before, everyone's needs are different in what they want in a lens. Do you want something that's fixed focus so you won't have to worry about it? Do you prefer a long zoom range on one camera that does it all? What length of zoom lens do you need? Do you really need one with interchangeable lenses?

The only way to pick the best of anything is to try them out. If you don't yet know what you need, then do your homework (we taught you how earlier) and see what's out there. Once you have an idea, you need to see what the lens can do.

The two most important items in a digital camera are its *charge-coupled device* (CCD) (the size and number of pixels) and the lens. When cameras were first developed in the nineteenth century, they were nothing more than a black box with a pin hole opening for light. The smaller the pin hole, the sharper the image on the film. No glass was needed.

We have graduated from black boxes to electronic black boxes with sophisticated, finely ground glass elements in which the light refracts, bends, and sends the image to the pickup device, the CCD. The better the glass (or plastic) the sharper and clearer the image will be. This is one area were you do not want to skimp.

With a point and shoot camera, you don't have much choice. When trying one on for size, if it's a fixed focus model, look at images up close, a slight distance away, and far away. Do the images look sharp at all three settings (wide, normal, and telephoto)? Although the lens doesn't move, the camera has to compensate for close-ups and distance shots. The old disposable point and shoot film cameras used a piece of plastic as a lens and most shots looked like they were done through Mylar.

If the camera has a fixed zoom lens, take several shots using the entire range of the zoom, from wide to telephoto. Every lens has a sweet spot where the image looks the best. Try to find it with the camera you're holding. If possible, try the same test outside in daylight. The f-stop will be smaller and you can see how the lens works in bright light.

If you desire a camera with interchangeable lenses, you obviously must try those lenses on the camera. If you already have them in your possession from your film days, you know they work, but how do they work on a digital camera?

Once again, test, test, and retest every lens to see which one is right for you. Hold an interchangeable lens up to the light and look through it. Are there any bubbles, scratches, smudges, or imperfections in the lens? This is impossible to check with a lens fixed on the camera. In film, you could always open the camera's back (with no film inside) and open the shutter to check the lens.

In any case, use the lens how you normally would for what you intend to do. If it passes the test, you now have a new friend that should be with you for a long time to come. Just keep it clean.

#27 How to Care for and Maintain Lenses

Whether your only lens is on a point and shoot camera or if you have a large collection, you need to care for and maintain your glass "eyes to the world."

Consider your lens as being your sensor's eye and protect it from scratches. Just about all digital cameras have lens covers that protect the lens when the camera is off. However, you still need to make sure you don't allow fingerprints or dust to get onto the surface of the lens while shooting.

In college if we ever got a fingerprint on a lens, we would have to let someone touch our eye with his or her thumb; it's the same principle.

Always turn your camera off when you're not using it and make sure the lens cover is in place. Be sure to keep your fingers away from the camera lens, as oily fingerprints on your lens are one of the worst setbacks you could have and can interfere with a nice sharp image. The oils will break down the coating on the lens element and will damage it if left there for an extended period of time.

Lens-cleaning tissue can be used to remove a smear, but roll the lens tissue (not your shirt, an old rag, or tissue) like a cigarette and use the end to gently brush away foreign debris. Blowing on the lens will send saliva everywhere.

When cleaning the lens becomes necessary, remove as much dust as possible by blowing on the lens with a syringe, an air bulb, or canned air. You can brush the lens lightly to remove any dust that remains after trying to use your air options. If you use a brush, use camel hair and don't touch the bristles with your fingers, as the oil on them will be transferred to the lens.

Lens cleaning can be divided into two schools. Never clean a lens dry because fine particles will scratch the surface when you rub it. Gently breathe on the lens to fog it and wipe in a circular motion without applying too much pressure. Some think that lens fluid is the best route, but most people use too much and the liquid will dissolve the glues in the lens's element over time.

It is also difficult to remove all the lens cleaner because it may leave a film. Experts can always tell when a lens has been cleaned with lens fluid because the telltale smear is always there. Sometimes a stubborn fingerprint or mark can only be removed with fluid, so use caution.

Apply the fluid to the lens tissue, not the lens itself where it collects and pools. Moderation is the key and less is always more.

Always protect your camera from moisture, whether when you're shooting outside in inclement weather or storing your camera for a period of time. Try to avoid shooting in a smoky environment, as smoke can coat your lens even faster than dust.

If the settings where you intend to take your pictures are inhospitable, depending on the digital camera you're using, you can use a plain glass filter (skylight filter 1A or 1B) on the front of your lens to protect it. Photographers using expensive cameras and lenses will leave the skylight filter on the lens all the time to reduce any potential damage. When using a filter, use a high-quality one. A cheap filter is like shooting through a piece of inexpensive glass and will degrade the sharpness of your lens. With a lower-end digital camera that hides the lens behind a cover, this may be unnecessary or even impossible to do.

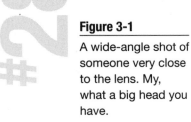

#28 How to Use a Wide-Angle Lens

If you only have one lens in your collection, a wide angle would be the most versatile. You may not always have the option of being able to back up to get the shot, and you can move in a little closer if you are seeing too much.

Let's imagine a realistic example. The museum we want to take a picture of is huge and we can't back up any farther to get the entire building in the shot. It's not a problem if we can either use our wide-angle selection on our point and shoot or if we have the capability of changing lenses on our higher-end digital camera.

Although wide-angle lenses are certainly useful, certain considerations must be made before shooting with them. If you're too close to your subject, you can expect to see some distortion in your picture. An example is shown in Figure 3-1.

If you're too close to the person you're photographing, objects that are much closer to the camera (such as a nose, knee, or hand) will

Figure 3-1

A wide-angle shot of someone very close to the lens. My, what a big head you have.

appear to be much larger than they actually are and tend to be unflattering. Try to stay farther away from your subject when using your wide-angle lens.

Wanting to distort the size of a child's head for a humorous ad, we used a wide-angle lens, got above her, and pointed the camera down. Her head filled the frame and her feet were tiny. Figure 3-2 shows the final result.

If an object such as your museum seems to be "falling away," it's because your camera is not parallel to the museum. Do everything possible to keep from tilting your camera when composing your picture. Look for vertical and horizontal lines in what you're shooting and try to line the camera up with them.

If necessary, try to shoot from a higher angle (take advantage of steps, a ladder, or anything else) to eliminate the need to tilt your camera upwards to get your shot. Figure 3-3 illustrates what a wide-angle lens does to the perspective of a building when shot from below.

A wide-angle lens tends to elongate the distance between objects. Someone could be standing next to someone else, but because of a wide-angle lens, it looks as though they are farther apart. The passenger sideview mirror in most cars is a great example of this. The mirror clearly reads, "objects may be closer than they appear." Because this mirror is wide angle to give you a better field of view when someone

Figure 3-2

Don't let this happen to your daughter.

Figure 3-3

Try this same lens with the Leaning Tower of Pisa.

#29

is about to pass, the distance a vehicle appears to be from you is deceiving.

Sit in the driver's seat of a car and have someone approach you from the rear on the passenger's side. Note that the distance he has to travel isn't too great for him to be at the mirror.

The museum pictures are going to be your challenge. A wide-angle lens for capturing a sporting event, parade, or any other picture opportunity that covers a large area is a great tool to have and use.

#29 How to Use a Normal Lens

In most situations, can we really call anything normal? In the case of a lens, a normal lens fits right in the middle between a wide-angle and a telephoto lens, without the expansion or compression of other lenses.

A normal lens is one that is usually supplied by a camera manufacturer at the time of purchase. Any lens is the eye of your camera, which captures the light used by your sensor to create the picture. A normal lens for a 35mm camera is typically 50 to 55mm depending upon the manufacturer. This sized lens allows you to see a normal field of view. You won't get everybody in a group shot and someone in the distance will still be difficult to distinguish. A normal lens here means "average," and it is the lens you'll normally use most of the time.

With a digital camera, the normal lens will vary with the CCD in the camera. Many digital camera manufacturers are not offering a normal lens; however, a standard lens with the new Nikon D100, for instance, is 28 to 90mm, which covers a normal lens' viewing area as well as wide-angle to medium telephoto lenses. A point and shoot such as the Nikon COOLPIX 775 is equipped with a 5.8 to 17.4mm lens, which is equivalent to a 35mm camera format of 38 to 115mm. We'll discuss how CCDs read the image seen through the lens differently than a 35mm in another solution.

The normal lens is an average focal length lens that can be used the vast majority of the time. Several years ago it was common for someone to purchase as a package a 35mm digital body with a 52mm lens, and add telephoto and wide-angle lenses as one's needs were determined. With the introduction several years ago of the zoom lens, it has changed the role and in some cases the need to have a normal lens.

Still, use a normal lens if you want to capture an image without distortion and get a medium point of view of the shot. You can't compare what the human eye sees to a normal lens (because we have two eyes and usually a camera has one lens). Most wide-angle lenses still aren't wide enough to see the panorama the eye sees. Just think how fortunate you are over a Cyclops. Figure 3-4 illustrates an image shot with a normal lens (55mm). Note the edges don't converge at the top and bottom of the image and the space between the subject and the background isn't compressed or expanded; it's normal.

#30 How to Use a Portrait Lens

Although you can rarely buy a lens called a *portrait lens*, if you take shots of people, formal or informal, it should be worth considering. A portrait lens is more telephoto than a normal lens, but less wide than a wide-angle one. When purchasing one, look for a low-range telephoto lens.

Point and shoot digital cameras may have a portrait setting or portrait mode that doesn't necessarily zoom in on the image. Instead, it

#30

Figure 3-4

An example of a normal picture taken with a normal lens

changes the focal distance so the subject (the person or object whose portrait you are taking) is sharply focused and the background is soft, making the eye go directly to the subject. People have learned to expect this in a portrait, and the look a normal lens gives is not the same.

Portraits are never shot with wide-angle lenses. People or pets need to be seen closer so we can identify with them (by looking at their eyes). When people paint portraits, they are always seen as if shot by a slightly telephoto lens. No portrait was painted seeing the subject from miles away.

A portrait lens is usually from 75 to 120mm. We have moved into the telephoto range, but not far enough to compress the image too much. This type of lens is more flattering on people because it slightly compresses larger facial features and makes the subject more attractive. We, however, are always behind the camera and no lens can make us look attractive.

When using a portrait lens, frame the subject in a medium shot from the waist up. It doesn't matter if he or she is standing or sitting. The camera should be far enough away to keep everything in that medium shot. Once again, the background will blur slightly because you will be focusing on the subject's eyes.

If the light level is low and your depth of field is narrow, make sure the eyes are in focus. If they appear soft, you do not have a soft focus

Figure 3-5

A portrait shot with a normal
lens

shot; you have an out of focus shot. With soft focus, everything is at the
same discrete level of sharpness, not just the eyes.

Figure 3-5 shows a portrait shot with a normal lens. The image is still
flattering and framed correctly, but it's too normal. Figure 3-6 used the
same subject, but this time with a portrait lens. Note how much better
the image looks with compressed features and a softened background.

#31 How to Use a Telephoto Lens

For those of you who want to get closer to the action while still keeping
your distance, the telephoto is the best lens to use. With a lower-end

Figure 3-6

A portrait shot with a portrait lens

digital camera, such as a point and shoot, you're basically dependent on the telephoto capabilities built into the camera.

With a digital camera that allows you to use interchangeable lenses, you have a wide variety of choices. It's often a good idea to use a tripod when shooting with a telephoto lens due to the size, weight, and speed of the lens. Some of the extremely large telephoto lenses (over 400mm) have a tripod mount of their own.

Your exposures will tend to be longer with a telephoto lens due to the distance the light has to travel inside the lens itself through all the elements. The faster the lens in light gathering, the more expensive it will be. A 200mm lens with an f-stop of 5.6 will cost a third of the same lens with a speed of F2.8. The glass is more expensive to refine and the end user will pay the price to get it, so if you want speed, it comes at a price.

It's important to be aware that a telephoto lens can cause distortion, but you can use that to your advantage. It may appear that the distance between your subjects or objects is closer or more compressed than how they actually are. Film students' favorite example of this is from the 1967 film *The Graduate* starring Dustin Hoffman (yes, he's that old). In one of the final scenes, he's running toward the camera to stop Elaine's wedding to the wrong man (not him). As he runs, he seems to get nowhere even though he is covering a large portion of ground. The director, Mike Nichols, chose to shoot this with a telephoto lens, 600mm to be exact. Even though Hoffman covered over 100 feet in the shot, the telephoto lens compressed the space to look as if he were running in place. The director achieved the frustration Hoffman was feeling by running but not really getting anywhere.

If you're shooting a large stationary object, if possible, open your camera's lens wider, which will separate your main object from the others by selectively focusing your shot. This, often done in portraits, softens the background and further distinguishes the subject.

If you're shooting smaller objects in a tabletop setting, you can eliminate any compression of your objects by spacing them farther apart. Be sure to view your image in the camera to make sure you've eliminated the distortion or compression problems. Your subjects may also appear closer with a telephoto lens than they would be with a wide-angle or normal setting.

When you watch the Olympics, photographers use the most extreme telephoto lenses, sometimes 1000mm. The expense of this lens is about the same as a car, but if you want to see pores and freckles, this lens can do it.

The telephoto lens or T setting on a camera is a must when shooting pictures of wildlife, sporting events, concerts, or speakers at a podium. The telephoto will allow you to get the picture you want without being a distraction by trying to get closer to your subject and consequently being a disturbance. Most of us are disturbed enough already. Figure 3-7 shows a scene shot with a telephoto lens, compressing everything.

#32 How to Use a Converter

Sometimes what you have is not quite good enough and you need a little more. Of course, we're referring to lenses, and a doubler will double the focal power of anything in front of it and a converter will widen or increase the telephoto power of a lens.

Figure 3-7

It's better to be compressed than depressed in a telephoto shot.

Let's look at a converter first. Coming in many sizes, the converter is rated in its magnification power and attaches behind the lens, almost like attaching a small mini-lens behind your lens. A .75x or .85x converter will widen the field of view of your lens. A .75x converter attached to a wide-angle 28mm lens will open it up to 21mm, allowing more people into the shot. If this same converter is placed in front of an extremely wide 15mm lens, you can do the math and figure out the millimeter range you will be shooting at (hint: divide 15 by .75). If you get too wide, the image will vignette or curve toward the top and bottom of the frame, close to that of a fish-eye lens.

The only drawbacks to using a wide-angle converter is that the image may distort, and the lens may cause shading around the edges of the frame. Other than that, you will now have a wider-angle lens.

1.0x, 1.5x, 2.0x, and 3.0x are the common magnification sizes or powers in converters. When put behind any lens, these will increase the magnification to that power. You can use these with wide-angle, normal, or telephoto lenses, and they will make them longer focal lengths —at a price. Anything above 1.0x will take a certain amount of light away from your image in f-stops. We have a 2.0x converter that doubles the magnification of our lenses (a 200mm becomes a 400mm), but it takes away two stops of light. Our F5.6 telephoto lens with the 2.0x converter now needs at least an F11 to capture an image. This is where a tripod comes in handy.

Some also say that a converter degrades the image slightly and a less expensive model will do that when increasing the power of your lens. Placed on the rear of your lens, the light now has to travel through the lens and through the converter to reach your CCD. If the converter's optics are inexpensive, your image quality will suffer. Buy only those that are compatible with your camera and avoid "no name" brands. A Kodak, Canon, or Nikon converter will work much better.

#33 How to Use a Doubler

A doubler, as its name implies, doubles the magnification of your shot. It is usually activated by a flip of a switch or a lever placed somewhere behind the lens to double its power.

Working with zoom or prime lenses, you can now have a more powerful arsenal of lenses with the addition of a converter or doubler. Figure 3-8 shows an image shot with a 210mm lens, and Figure 3-9 shows an image with a 2x converter attached, making it a 420mm lens.

#34 How 35mm and Digital Lenses Differ

Although the lenses many be the same millimeter range and easily fit on your 35mm film and digital cameras, the image your digital camera takes probably will be more telephoto than if you used it on your film unit. Why is this?

Figure 3-8

An icy tree shot at 210mm

Figure 3-9

A 2x converter took most of the light and we want it back.

Digital cameras have a CCD that isn't exactly the same size as the film plane in a 35mm camera. The size of the CCD will have an impact on the millimeter range your camera actually reads, theoretically changing the millimeter range of your lens.

As an example, both the Fuji S2 Pro and the Nikon D100 digital cameras' CCDs add a magnification power of 1.5 times to the lens in front, because the CCD is one and a half times smaller than a 35mm film camera's gate. Therefore, a normal 50mm film camera lens on either of these two digital cameras will in fact be a 75mm, slightly more telephoto lens.

This extra magnification is helpful in most shooting instances because if you have interchangeable lenses, they are all now more telephoto. That monster 500mm is now a 750mm and the 70mm to 300mm zoom's range has changed to 105mm to 450mm. The range or zoom ratio doesn't change, just the beginning and ending points. This may save you money when looking for new telephoto lenses; they have been converted for you.

The real drawback occurs in the wide-angle range where none of your old lenses are quite as wide. That pristine 20mm wide-angle lens is now 30mm and no longer quite as nice. Most people prefer having more telephoto than width capabilities. If you need a digital camera that is exactly the same as a film camera, good luck. They are almost impossible to find. Each one will have a factor greater than one.

You can buy lenses built just for your digital camera with a wider angle and they may be really wide film lenses that were modified for your digital camera. The point and shoot cameras may not even have a millimeter marking on the lens and you're stuck with that range. There is no sense trying to equate that to what a film camera's lens might see. The numbers we gave you were just for comparison purposes if you can use your film lens on your digital camera. If you can't, don't worry about it.

If some feel this is a drawback, it is the only one that digital has. A digital device is superior to film in every way. Now you can really see what people look like up close.

Chapter 4

Filters

#35 How Filters Work

As the name implies, filters change or suppress the light entering your lens. With a filter, you can achieve almost any effect you desire. In this chapter, you will learn how to use diffusion filters, how to use color correction filters, and how to use special effects filters.

#36 How to Use Diffusion Filters

The old joke about being slightly diffused works well in this solution. Sometimes you want the image to be a little soft rather than sharp and clear. A diffusion filter is the best way of accomplishing this, because it affects the entire image. If you just diffuse the lighting, you have soft lighting, but the picture remains sharp.

Diffusion filters are most frequently used when shooting portraits. These filters soften the shot so that it is appealing to your subject as well as flattering. After all, who doesn't want to appear to have the perfect complexion?

The nice thing about diffusing an image is that you don't actually need to go out and purchase a filter that you may only use a few times a year. Something as simple as a nylon stocking in front of the lens will work or a plain glass filter with a small amount of petroleum jelly will also do just fine.

With the stocking approach, use a high-quality black stocking to keep the flesh tones normal. If using petroleum jelly (such as Vaseline), make sure you use a small amount and smear it on a piece of glass or skylight filter. Never put anything on the lens other than a filter.

With digital cameras where you don't have the option of using an actual filter, these makeshift diffusers may be your answer. Shooting through frosted glass, plastic wrap (such as Saran

Wrap), or a glass will also diffuse the image. The thicker the object you shoot through, the stronger the diffusion.

If none of these options are available, you can soften your image after the shoot using a photo image editor. It may be best to apply these effects after first capturing the image. If you shoot with diffusion and later decide you no longer want it, it will be very difficult to remove with software.

A diffusion filter can provide an appearance similar to a fog filter; however, we don't recommend using a fog filter when shooting a portrait, unless the person you are shooting is foggy in real life. Figure 4-1 shows someone shot with a black stocking. Figure 4-2 shows the same person shot with petroleum jelly on a filter.

#37 How to Use Color Correction Filters

Light in digital photography is measured in color temperature by degrees Kelvin. Daylight is 5,600 degrees Kelvin and tungsten light is 3,200 degrees Kelvin. These are the two norms but rarely does anyone shoot in perfect daylight (no clouds) or tungsten light (perfectly balanced at 3,200 degrees Kelvin rather than incandescent).

Color correction is basically a way to change the balance of colors in an image, often to improve the accuracy of the photo. Color correction can also compensate for deficiencies in the color separation and

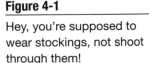

Figure 4-1

Hey, you're supposed to wear stockings, not shoot through them!

Figure 4-2

Pass the jelly, please—the petroleum jelly. Notice the features are softened or blurred slightly.

printing process. Is the shot too blue or too orange (too much daylight and tungsten respectively)?

It's not important that you memorize the color temperature of every source of light. Digital cameras have made it easier by having a little "sun" option to set for daylight shooting. This adjusts color balance for daylight and a "lightbulb" option for shooting indoor shots by balancing the color temperature for indoor shooting. But as we said earlier, you are rarely in a situation where you have pure daylight or tungsten. That's where you need to color correct.

The digital camera's white-balancing provision corrects filtration issues that were normally taken care of by traditional filters. The digital cameras have less need for filter attachments than conventional film cameras. We had to carry a box of orange and blue filters to compensate for the changing color temperature of the light with our film cameras. Now white balancing will do that for you.

You may still want to use filters for special effects if your digital camera allows you to. Depending on the camera, you can use a color correction filter to warm up or cool off a picture without adjusting the white-balance control. We've warmed up skin tones by white balancing on a light blue card instead of white. It tricks the camera's white-balance circuitry into thinking that 2,900 degrees Kelvin is normal tungsten light (3200°) and therefore makes the shot more orange colored or warmer.

White balancing may not compensate completely for certain fluorescent lights (around 4,200 degrees Kelvin). Fluorescent filters can color correct for this type of lighting, but it depends on the type of light (cool white deluxe or daylight). By underexposing an image while adding a slight amount of blue filtration (an 80A filter), you can simulate nighttime, but you will also need to use a smaller f-stop (possibly several f-stops) and add an 80A filter. Conversely, a Coral filter will warm up the shot, whereas an orange 85 filter is too much. You will want a subtle color temperature decrease.

If you determine that your shot is too blue, possibly the camera had been set to an indoor setting when shooting an outdoor scene under daylight. If your shot is too red, unless badly sunburned, the subject was shot in a daylight setting while indoors under tungsten light. Both images are correctable with software packages.

#38 How to Use Special Effects Filters

Special effects are any type of photographic effect that is unusual or out of the ordinary. If you're looking for a change from the ordinary, several things are available that you can try.

When taking your picture, various filters can be used to avoid problems or create an interesting image. A polarizing filter can help eliminate glare on a window of a house or building and is especially helpful when taking pictures of an automobile. By being able to see the glare being eliminated by rotating the filter and checking your image on your digital camera, you can be certain that you have achieved the desired effect. Occasions may occur, however, when you want a slight glare present in order to indicate that the car you're photographing for a print ad does in fact have a windshield.

When shooting silverware or chrome objects, the polarizing filter can eliminate reflections. If you're shooting a portrait, you may want to consider using a diffusion filter that will soften the image to provide a flattering portrait. If you don't have a diffusion filter in your camera bag, it's no big deal. A piece of a nylon stocking held over the front of the lens can give you the same effect. Of course, always check your image in the camera to make sure it's not too soft where it begins to look out of focus.

To avoid changing the color temperature of your image, a black stocking can be used. A natural stocking or "nude" pantyhose can warm up the image, and white (nurse-type) stockings can create a blue look. Black acts as a neutral density and does not change the color temperature. Cheaper stockings will tear, so get the best you can afford and they will be free of defects and last much longer. Victoria's Secret and Fredrick's of Hollywood are the best we've found. When you're finished using them, they also make great gifts (to other photographers, of course).

You can also use the aforementioned fog filers, especially when shooting landscapes, as well as star effect filters that add sunbursts to your picture. Neutral-density filters cut down the amount of light when shooting at a beach or a snow-covered landscape on a sunny day.

Check with your local camera store for other special effects filters. These are not something you will use every day but are nice to have when the need or occasion arises. Naturally, you can also create special effects after the fact using your image editor software.

Chapter 5

What Kind of Pictures Can I Take?

#39 What Kind of Pictures Can I Take?

This chapter discusses all the different types of images you can take with your digital camera. The solutions include how to shoot close-ups and formal portraits while using the portrait mode feature on your camera. The chapter will also discuss how to shoot large groups, how to get great action photographs, how to keep the image sharp when panning the camera, and how to adjust and control shutter speed. Further topics include how to determine the correct aperture selection, how to use the camera in automatic as well as manual mode, and how to use auto-focus more effectively. Using the preferred or priority settings on your camera, shooting in macro mode, using diopters, and how to use extension tubes or bellows are also discussed. You'll also learn how to use backlight effectively, how to shoot in limited light as well as bright sunlight, how to photograph the moon, how to shoot fireworks, and how to determine the correct length for opening the shutter when shooting time exposures.

#40 How to Shoot Close-Ups

Remember the old TV commercial, "The closer you get, the better she looks?" That may not always apply in close-up photography, but times will occur when you need to get up close and personal with your digital camera.

When shooting close-ups, always try to use a tripod. With a tripod, you don't need to be concerned about your shutter speed. Most people have a difficult time with shutter speeds slower than 1/30 of a second. They tend to do bad things that visibly blur the image, basically moving or breathing. A tripod also gives you the opportunity to compose your picture while reviewing it in the viewfinder, allowing you to make changes to your composition. The camera isn't going to move during the exposure, especially with the use of a cable release. The cable release (an external triggering device to fire the shutter attached to a cable) is important because you're never actually touching the camera itself, thus eliminating the chance of banging it.

If a tripod is not available, try to find something sturdy enough to rest the camera on while taking your picture. If you don't have a cable release, it's possible you could compose the picture and use the self-timer (if available), which will eliminate touching the camera to begin the exposure. As mentioned earlier, very few people have the ability to hold a camera steady using a shutter speed less than 1/15, or even 1/30 of a second.

On many cameras you'll have a close-up setting or in some cases a macro setup plus a self-timer. Some newer cameras have the option of setting the self-timer to either 3 or 10 seconds. Be sure to use the smallest f-stop to maximize the depth of field, unless you want to highlight a particular part of the picture. If you were photographing a bee on a flower and wanted the bee to stand out because the flower was not fully in bloom, you'd want to use an f-stop that would focus on the bee and allow the background to be soft or blurred.

Depending on the camera's options, you may have the ability to change lenses, use close-up filters, and attach adapters or a bellows extension. Obviously, the higher-end (more expensive) cameras provide more options than a basic yet reliable lower-end camera, but with either one, you should have the capability to view a close-up image.

Remember, when you shoot digital you always have the option of manipulating and editing the image with many different types of software. Trying to light a close-up with artificial light, such as a flash, is extremely difficult because your camera is normally very close to the subject. Often you can bounce light off a white piece of paper (or actually anything white that you can find) and allow that light to fall onto your subject, creating a soft light. A soft light can be considered to be any light that is not directed at your subject.

Overhead fluorescent lighting or incandescent lighting can cause problems with color shifts in your pictures. Some of these color shifts can be corrected by using a color correction filter on the camera, and some digital cameras give you the choice of selecting the type of lighting conditions you'll be shooting under (signified by a lightbulb icon for indoors and a sun icon for outdoors).

If you need to shoot inside, take advantage of any daylight you have to help light your subject. If you have a window nearby and can move your subject, do so and keep in mind that you may still want to bounce some of the sunlight onto your subject. Flashes are daylight balanced, so the color temperature of indoor and outdoor scenes will be consistent.

If you're shooting outdoors, let the sun do the work for you. Too much sunlight can wash out (make your image too light), so you may need to shield your subject from the sun slightly. Since digital photography is immediate, you can see what type of adjustments you need to make by taking a look at the image in your camera. Continue to make your adjustments and review them until you feel you have the best possible picture. Then take it before somebody changes their mind.

#41   How to Shoot Formal Portraits

Just the mention of the word "formal" sends chills down most people's spines. In this case, formal means the type of portrait taken, not necessarily the clothing the subject may be wearing.

The first question that should come to mind when someone asks you to shoot a formal portrait should be, "What is the picture for?" For example, will it be a business portrait where you need to show an executive in his or her work environment? It could possibly be a doctor or veterinarian in his or her office with a wall full of credentials (a possible lighting problem with glass reflections), an engineer reviewing a blueprint (a large contrast range between the paper and what the person may be wearing), or a computer user or at his or her workstation (don't show the computer screen).

This is an area where digital image capturing can bring the most to the table. Many times executives are too busy to travel to a studio, so you're limited to shooting in their work environment, or more commonly called their turf. Although these areas are functional, they don't always lend themselves to a great setting for a formal portrait. Often, distractions will abound.

Your main challenge is to get the best facial expression, lighting, mood, and, in general, the most flattering image possible. Keep in mind that along with *any* image manipulation, the individual should approve the idea and the final image. You may want to consider a full-length body shot to better display an individual's personality. If a head and shoulders portrait is what you're after, that should not be a problem.

This type of portrait allows you to select a lens that will cover the area required and you can also eliminate or blur as much of the background as you desire. When you're doing any digital manipulation or enhancement afterwards, you'll have much less background to deal with, saving headaches later.

With any portrait, pose your subjects in a natural and relaxed way. You don't want them looking directly into the camera. The subjects should turn their shoulders to the point where a portion of the back is visible. Have them looking over their shoulders back into the camera. This can be a right or left turn.

Shoot, shoot, and shoot some more, reviewing as you go along. Often your subjects will be more relaxed as you take more pictures, especially if they've had a chance to review them with you as you go along. They may notice subtle things and decide what they might like to change. Whether it be the expression, hair, make-up (as applicable), arm or hand position, or wrinkles in clothing, now is the time to fix it.

Although a formal portrait, the subject's arms should be slightly bent. If people like the idea of having a hand placed under the chin, the hands need to be somewhat attractive (or at least not take away from the picture). The hands should also not effect or block the face in any way. Ask your subject for his or her opinion and don't be hesitant to offer suggestions, even though they may not be what the person wants to hear.

Ultimately, it's the subject's decision and it's your job to make them happy (hopefully not at your expense). Give them the images (with a watermark or indicate proof for your protection) so they can get input from others. This also is a good way to advertise at no expense to you. Figure 5-1 shows a formal portrait, just like one you would get professionally. This one was shot with a plain background, a posed subject, and an inexpensive camera.

#42 How to Shoot in the Portrait Format

Another way of describing the portrait format would be the vertical image. If you hold the camera vertically rather than horizontally, you are in the portrait mode. When should you use it?

When determining the composition of your picture, consider what you want to be your focal point. If you're out in the woods with your digital camera and you notice a small waterfall, what do you want to see in addition to the water flowing over the rocks? If nothing to the left or right of the waterfall is interesting, you'll want to photograph it as a ver-

Figure 5-1

A formal portrait shot with a nonprofessional camera.

tical or portrait. However, if whitetail deer were on both sides of the stream, you may want to reconsider a vertical picture (and don't rush home to get your rifle; that's a different type of shooting).

The format of the picture depends on what you personally want to see or show. With some objects, it's obvious how they should be photographed. If you notice an eagle sitting on top of a telephone pole (for whatever reason), you certainly would want to turn your camera to a vertical position and shoot in a portrait format. Of course, your other option is to shoot the picture as a landscape or a horizontal shot, which would probably move you back into the next county or necessitate the use of a wide-angle lens, causing you to end up with unnecessary distortion of everything in your image.

Many people we know, when faced with a split decision on how to shoot, will shoot in landscape style with the idea that you can always crop to portrait. Don't be afraid to turn the camera on its side. Sometimes this is a better way to capture the image. Figure 5-2 shows an example of portrait format.

Figure 5-2

An example of the vertical or portrait format

#42

#43 How to Photograph Large Groups

What do you do if you're asked to shoot a large group of people (besides telling them to squeeze together)? You should organize the group into a pleasing pattern, rather than the usual police lineup.

The key to getting a really good picture of a large group is the word of the day: composition. With a large group of 100 people, for example, a number of issues need to be addressed. The first question that should come to mind is, where are we going to find the space to take a picture of this many people? Unless you have access to a satellite, in most cases, the picture should be taken outside. This has both advantages and disadvantages. One disadvantage is that you're at the mercy of the weather.

It could rain on the day of the scheduled shoot, but on the bright side, an overcast sky would be helpful because of its even, diffused lighting. This may sound odd, but on a sunny day, the harsh light from the sun can work against you. A full sun is going to create shadows on their faces. Depending on the direction of the sun (the time of day), faces may become washed out or too light on one side. An additional problem is that people are going to have a tendency to squint due to the brightness of the sun.

Did you ever wonder why John Wayne was always squinting? Under his 10-gallon hat, a 24,000-watt movie light or silver reflector was used to light his face when the brim of his hat was creating a shadow. You can always ask your subject to remove his hat, but if it's John Wayne, *you* do it!

If you must shoot in bright sunlight, try to get your people outside a few minutes prior to the scheduled time of the shoot. This extra time outside will allow their eyes some time to adjust to the sun.

We had a shoot some time ago with Charles Bronson. The director requested that we turn off the arc lighting for a few minutes so he wouldn't squint. Unfortunately, Mr. Bronson squints indoors and out, light or no light.

Even though we're shooting digital, we don't want to spend hours on the computer trying to create eyes for half the group who happened to be squinting. Taxidermists are specialists at this, but with humans, an ounce of prevention . . .

As the person responsible for taking a pleasing shot of the group, you should be prepared for a number of things. Take advantage of a hill or incline, which will enable you to tier the people so you'll see everyone's

face. Bleachers are ideal and can normally be rented or borrowed from a local organization. If these options aren't available, try your local fire department. With a small donation, they may be willing to allow you to get into the bucket of one of their trucks (insurance issues could be a problem here) and get a good shot from a higher angle. Depending on the height of a nearby building, taking your shot from the roof could also be an option. As with any digital shoot, any background or foreground issues can be taken care of later on your computer.

Let's say we get lucky and we've been requested to take a picture indoors with adequate space for a group this size. This should be a piece of cake compared to an outdoor shoot. It will eliminate some of the issues we've discussed, but you still have a lot to consider. If you're shooting at a school or in a hotel, you'll have either bleachers or risers at your disposal. With access to the bleachers, you've got it made. If using risers, you have the option of having people standing on the risers, another row of people standing in front of the risers, a third row seated in front of the risers, and, if necessary, a fourth row kneeling in front of those seated.

You should arrive well before the shoot so all necessary arrangements can be made, including test exposures capturing the area you anticipate to cover. Review your images in the camera so your exposure will be one less item you'll need to consider when you have the group ready for the picture.

#44 How to Arrange People in a Group Photo

In order to arrange the group for the picture, you must be in control. Let them know that it's important to listen to your instructions because you take pride in your group photos and you want this to be one they will be especially proud of. With this large group, begin with the back row. The tallest person should be located in the middle with the two next-tallest people on either side, and continue until the row is filled.

When the back row is full, do the same with the remaining rows until everyone is in place. In order to keep a nice tight group, ask the people to turn their right shoulder toward the camera if they're on your left side looking at the rest of the group. For the people on the right side, ask them to turn their left shoulder toward the camera. This may seem somewhat "military style," but it works for any size group.

You should ask the people in the front row on your left to place their hands on their thighs and cross their right foot over their left. Those on your right should cross their left foot over their right. This may sound confusing, but it makes a much better image.

Finally, when it's time to shoot, take multiple images. Inform the group that with so many people you need to take numerous exposures so that you'll have a couple really nice shots where everyone is looking toward the camera with their eyes open. If the situation warrants, tell them at least three jokers in the group will close their eyes the second the shutter snaps. Explain that you must take several pictures because of them. This may also cause a few more smiles.

Shoot as quickly as possible after your flash recycles, as these people have hopefully been very cooperative and patient throughout this experience. After you've taken your last exposure, thank them for making your job easier (hopefully, this will be a true statement). Tell them that the other word for taking a picture is "shoot," so if anyone causes trouble, that's just what you'll do. Invite them to look into the camera at the images if they would like. Figure 5-3 illustrates an example of a nicely framed large group photo.

After the shoot is over and everyone has left the room, be sure to clean up the area and get everything back to the way it was prior to the photo session. Most importantly, if you have any input in determining when to do the group photo, shoot before cocktails!

Figure 5-3

A large mob (or group) shot

#45 How to Shoot Action Photographs

Photographing any moving object can be a challenge, but it doesn't have to be difficult. Depending on the event, you may be limited as far as how close you can get to the action. If you have no restrictions, take advantage of the opportunity to move around and shoot from various distances, angles, and positions.

High-angle shots would work for a sporting event involving several players, such as baseball or soccer. A lower angle would be effective when taking a picture of a football player being tackled in front of you. Try to be aware of others who are also watching the event and don't obstruct their view. The key to getting a good action picture that is not blurry or unsharp is to shoot at the highest possible shutter speed that the camera allows.

Depending on your camera, if available, adjust your ISO or film speed to the highest possible setting. Some digital cameras have an action mode that will automatically calculate the best exposure while using a higher shutter speed. If your camera has a shutter priority mode, use it and set the shutter speed to the highest one available, which will typically be 1/500 or 1/1000 of a second. Some higher-end cameras also have shutter speeds at the 1/2000 or 1/4000 of a second. Something this fast will freeze any action.

It's also helpful to position yourself so that the moving object is coming toward the direction of the camera. If this is possible, and if lighting conditions are not the best, you can use a slower shutter speed, because the apparent motion is less. To help stop action that's moving directly across your path, you can also *pan* with the action by moving the camera in the same direction as the object is moving. When you do this, the background will be blurry due to the movement of the camera, but the foreground subject will be sharp. You've all seen examples of this in pictures where a car or motorcycle is in crisp focus and the background is a blur of color. These pictures can be pleasing and they are not a typical shot the average photographer may shoot. You're actually showing the motion and the picture has a taste of creativity.

On the contrary, if you just snap the fast-moving action without panning the camera with the action, the background will be sharp and more defined, and the foreground subject may blur slightly depending on your shutter speed. With digital cameras, you can easily check your shot and see if it's what you really want.

Some digital cameras have a sequence mode that allows you to take a series of pictures in a very short time frame. The sequence mode is ideal for capturing images at an event where the action happens quickly, such as a car race or a basketball game. If you're familiar with a sport or event, try to anticipate what might happen next, which will better prepare you to get the best picture possible. With digital cameras, you can shoot up to eight frames a second, all with a shutter speed of 1/2000 of a second or faster. People have already shot over 400 still images during the course of a basketball game and stored them in the camera.

You can also use your aperture to control the amount of sharpness you want in the picture. For instance, if you wanted to freeze the action of a tennis player and not have the background in focus, you could open the aperture to F4 or F5.6, again depending on the amount of light available.

Another method to achieve the same effect without the open aperture is to use a longer lens to compress the subject against the background. Any lens above 135mm will accomplish this feat, with longer lenses (400mm, 600mm, and 1000mm) compressing the action even further.

During the Winter Olympics, photographers use 1000mm lenses, supported by tripods, to freeze the action, often with an f-stop of F16. Depending on the amount of light available, you have the option of shutter speed: the faster the shutter, the more light needed. With f-stops, the larger the iris opening, the less defined the background or depth of field is. With the focal length of the lens, the more telephoto the lens, the more compressed the image. Figure 5-4 shows an

Figure 5-4

Freezing the action with a high shutter speed makes any subject look better.

example of frozen action in the summer. Try a combination of each of these and see what works best for you.

#46 How to Maintain Sharpness by Panning the Camera

As mentioned previously, panning is a little trick to help you keep fast-moving objects sharp and clear in the frame. Achieved by following the action with the camera, a racehorse can now be easily identifiable against a greatly blurred background.

This trick can take a little practice, so review your images as you're shooting to make sure you're getting the sharpness you want for your subject. If your goal is to freeze action that's taking place in front of you, move or pan the camera in the same direction as the subject's motion and take the picture while following your subject.

Going against everything you've been told since day one, forget about holding the camera firmly and stationary while taking a picture. Yes, your camera is actually moving while framing and taking the picture, just like using a motion video camera, but when you follow the moving subject with the camera, you're reducing the amount of apparent motion so a slower shutter speed can still freeze the image. Also, since you'll be following the subject and taking your shot, the background will be blurry and make the subject appear sharper.

Panning the camera is a necessity, especially when photographing fast-moving objects crossing your path. Try panning a few times as objects pass in front of you without actually taking a picture just to get a feel for what you need to do and when. It's a challenge, but the result is very effective.

Figure 5-5 shows a racecar that has been frozen in time by panning the camera with the action. Video camera people do this all the time when shooting sporting events. Now it's your turn to accomplish the same thing with your digital still camera.

#47 How to Adjust and Control Shutter Speed

Sometimes you want more control when capturing your digital images than just pointing and shooting. Depending on the amount of light available, if you control your shutter speed, you can open it when letting in more light is the answer, and close it using a faster shutter speed when you need freeze to the action.

Figure 5-5

The car hasn't stalled, just the background.

Whatever the reason, you need to know how a shutter functions to best utilize it. Just like on a film camera, the shutter is the electronic door that opens and closes at a predetermined speed to let light fall onto your *charge-coupled device* (CCD). The faster it opens, the more light it allows in. If the shutter remains open for longer periods of time, more light will strike the surface of the CCD.

The shutter speeds on a digital camera are the same as those of a film camera. Anything slower than 1/30 of a second demands a very steady hand or tripod (1/15 of a second and slower). Outdoor speeds like 1/60, 1/125, 1/250, and faster will freeze the action in sharp detail by letting in less light. Figure 5-6 illustrates how time can stand still with a faster shutter speed.

Speeds faster than 1/500 of a second are only used in extreme circumstances, whereas a shutter speed of 1/8 of a second or slower is used when you need the shutter to stay open as long as necessary. Figure 5-7 shows an extremely slow shutter speed, which is evident by the blurring of the motion.

When photography was in its infancy, subjects had to sit in front of the camera for several minutes without moving because of extremely slow film stocks. That's the main reason why you never see anyone smiling in a turn of the century photograph. Nobody could sit still and

#47

Figure 5-6

A moment frozen in time because of a faster shutter speed

Figure 5-7

A slow shutter speed and blurry features (or feathers in this case)

hold a smile that long. Any movement would end up being blurry. Images of cars on streets were devoid of people because the humans moved too fast for the long exposure. Luckily, cameras have come a long way since then.

Assuming you have the option of controlling your shutter speed on your digital camera, and if it has a Shutter Priority setting, select the shutter speed you'd like to use. Your digital camera will automatically select an aperture when it is set on Shutter Priority, because that's what the priority is. The higher the shutter speed you select, the less depth of field you'll have as the aperture will open wider, allowing more illumination.

If a warning light appears after you set the camera to the fastest shutter speed, change to the next-fastest setting because there may not be enough light available at your highest shutter speed.

Slowing the shutter speed down should still allow you to freeze any action with the light available. Keep in mind as you adjust the shutter speed to a higher setting that your aperture will open up to compensate for less light entering through the lens.

F-stops and shutter speed work hand in hand. As you increase your shutter speed, the f-stops will open wider to let more light onto the CCD. With a slower shutter speed and enough existing light, you can stop down your lens and increase your depth of field. Very few times in life do you have this much control over anything. Enjoy it while you can.

#48 How to Determine Aperture Selection

The other side of the coin when exposing an image is to adjust the aperture or f-stop instead of the shutter speed. The aperture you select will determine two different vital items.

The first will resolve how much of your image will be in focus or your depth of field, and the other, how much light is entering the camera during your exposure. When making an aperture selection, keep in mind that the smaller the lens opening, the more depth of field you'll have. It's amazing how deep your focus is at a high f-stop like F16. Just remember the fighter jet (F-16) and you know you can travel far with focus. Table 5-1 shows your depth of field at a given f-stop. Notice how it sharply increases the smaller the aperture.

The larger your aperture, the less depth of field you'll have, and you'll need to focus carefully to make sure the main subject of your image is sharp or in focus. As mentioned earlier, the subject's eyes are critical to keep in focus with a narrow depth of field. Even if the tip of the nose is slightly blurry, the eyes need to be sharp.

Many people shooting with their digital camera will let it determine the aperture settings, but if you can manually select the aperture, it will add to what you can do creatively. If you want a narrow or deep depth of field, select the aperture you want and let the camera determine the shutter speed. This is useful in portraits where you want a narrow depth of field. Set the f-stop at F4 and let the camera select the shutter speed. In the manual mode, you'll need to set both the aperture and the shutter speed.

The largest lens opening is typically F2, F1.8, or F1.4 and the smallest is F22 or F32, with each increasing number increment admitting half

TABLE 5-1   Depth of Field Guide, Lens Focal Length – 50mm

Lens Focus (feet)	F2 Near Far	F2.8 Near Far	F4 Near Far	F5.6 Near Far	F8 Near Far	F11 Near Far	F16 Near Far	F22 Near Far
50	30'11" 130'3"	26'10" 361'9"	22'5" INF.	18'5" INF.	14'6" INF.	11'6" INF.	8'6" INF.	6'7" INF.
25	19'2" 36'1"	17'6" 43'10"	15'6" 64'7"	13'6" 174'3"	11'3" INF.	9'4" INF.	7'4" INF.	5'10" INF.
15	12'8" 18'4"	11'11" 20'2"	11'0" 23'8"	9'11" 30'9"	8'8" 55'5"	7'6" 0'8"	6'2" INF.	5'0" INF.
10	8'11" 11'5"	8'7" 12'1"	8'1" 13'2"	7'6" 15'2"	6'9" 19'4"	6'0" 29'8"	5'1" 244'7"	4'4" INF.
8	7'4" 8'10"	7'1" 9'3"	6'8" 9'11"	6'4" 11'0"	5'9" 13'0"	5'3" 16'11"	4'6" 33'11"	3'11" INF.
6	5'7" 6'6"	5'5" 6'8"	5'3" 7'0"	5'0" 7'6"	4'8" 8'5"	4'4" 9'11"	3'10" 13'11"	3'4" 27'0"
5	4'9" 5'4"	4'7" 5'5"	4'6" 5'8"	4'3" 6'0"	4'0" 6'7"	3'9" 7'5"	3'5" 9'6"	3'0" 14'1"
4	3'10" 4'2"	3'9" 4'3"	3'8" 4'5"	3'6" 4'7"	3'4" 4'11"	3'2" 5'5"	2'11" 6'5"	2'8" 8'2"
3	2'11" 3'1"	2'10" 3'2"	2'10" 3'3"	2'9" 3'4"	2'8" 3'6"	2'6" 3'9"	2'4" 4'2"	2'2" 4'10"
2	1'11" 2'1"	1'11" 2'1"	1'11" 2'1"	1'11" 2'2"	1'10" 2'2"	1'9" 2'3"	1'8" 2'5"	1'7" 2'8"

the light and each decrease allowing twice as much light. You'll probably have an aperture selection of F32, F22, F16, F11, F8, F5.6, F4, F2, and F1.8. You may also have settings between f-stops, which are half-stop adjustments. The notch between F8 and F11 is a half-stop, letting in more light than F8 but less than F11.

Aperture selection is based on lighting conditions and the depth of field you want your finished image to have. Try shooting at several different apertures and review them in the camera until you get the desired look you're after.

#49

#49 How to Use Auto-Focus Effectively

If your camera has auto-focus capabilities, should you use it or rely on focusing the shot manually? This is something that professionals rarely admit they do, but with the speed of today's auto-focus lenses, we just can't do it as quickly or as accurately as the auto-focus.

The sophisticated focusing system in cameras is unbelievable. High-end cameras can actually sense a moving image and keep it in focus instead of the operator trying to rack through the focus as it moves. Using auto-focus, a basketball player can run, jump in the air for a lay-up, and land on the court, and the player will stay in focus all the time.

When we are shooting sporting events where the action is happening quickly, our hand-to-eye coordination isn't as accurate as the camera's sensors. We will still expose the shot manually but usually allow the digital camera to handle the focus. Figure 5-8 shows a fast-action example where the camera was tracking the subject using auto-focus. This still would be possible with manual focus, but too many other factors may be taking up the photographer's attention.

Figure 5-8

An example of an auto-focus shot that may have been difficult to get without it

If your camera has auto-focus, it may also have a manual mode. Times may occur when the auto-focus won't work and instead the camera hunts for a correct focus by constantly rolling the lens in and out. This usually happens if too little light exists and the camera is having difficulty deciding what to focus on. This may also happen if you're too close to the subject and the camera just isn't capable of getting the shot.

In all other scenarios, the auto-focus feature is unbeatable. With the Nikon D100, in a fraction of a second, the camera electronically finds the mark even if it is moving and focuses to crystal clarity. As we humans age, it becomes more difficult to focus precisely and the camera can usually do a better job much faster. Does that mean when we approach 50 we have to dispose of all our manual lenses? Instead, we should think of just grinding them down to make better glasses for us.

The Canon D60 has a great auto-focus capability, but when shooting in rapid succession, we find it easier to switch to the manual mode and make any minute adjustments ourselves. Once again, we are the ones with the brains and the camera will focus on what it thinks is correct.

Using this same digital camera on a legal video shoot, we had to capture a patient's scar from an accident. Focused in an extreme close-up on his neck, the auto-focus constantly centered on his Adam's apple and left the scar directly below slightly out of focus. Although the two were less than a half-inch apart, the depth of field was extremely narrow using a 400mm lens. Having to resort to manual focus, we captured the images and had them enlarged for the client.

The best advice is to practice with the auto-focus feature and see if it works in your situations. You can always revert back to the manual mode, but at least you gave it a try.

#50 How to Use Diopters

In this solution, you get two for the price of one. Diopters can be used in front of the camera on the lens to get really close to something as well as on the viewfinder to magnify the image, allowing the user to remove his or her glasses or contacts to take the shot. In this solution, we'll discuss how to use both. A diopter is a ground piece of glass that magnifies the image — much like what a magnifying glass does.

Using a diopter in front of the camera's lens gets you extremely close to the action without the need for a macro lens. Of course, this only works with lenses that will accept screw-on filters, so most point and shoot models will be left out in the cold.

Diopters are pieces of glass that have been ground with a magnification factor. They are purchased or rented in factors of -3, -2, -1, 0, +1, +2, and +3. Very much like reading glasses purchased in stores, the higher the number, the greater the magnification, with 0 being almost clear glass.

As an example, let's say you want to shoot an extreme close-up of a brochure on a copy stand. The camera is mounted to a fixed tripod and the brochure is on a table below the lens. The closer you move to the brochure, the stronger or greater the plus number you'll need on the diopter. With a +3, you literally are only a few millimeters from what you're photographing. For cameras that don't have macro capabilities, a diopter will get you close to what you're photographing.

If you are doing a lot of copy or extreme close-up work, purchasing a set of diopters may be best; however, with occasional use, a rental set would do nicely. If you want to shoot your stamp collection, the same diopter would work for everything. But if you are shooting mounted insects, for example, various strength diopters are better, because some insects are larger than others and the camera needs to be pulled farther away.

Focusing with a diopter is usually accomplished by moving the camera closer or farther away until the image is sharp. Adjusting the focus (like a macro) rarely works with a diopter attached to the lens. If you prefer to see everything clearly without wearing your glasses or contacts, a diopter on the viewfinder will allow you to see things clearly with your naked eye—with a few drawbacks.

Everyone's eyes are different so you will need a different diopter power than the next person. If several people are using the same camera, the diopter must be changed for each person because no two people see alike. In addition, you must get a diopter that exactly fits the digital camera you are using. With over 30 models of digital cameras from Nikon alone, 21 different screw mounts may exist for your diopter. In short, you need to buy a diopter that fits your camera exactly.

If you are farsighted, you may need a -2 diopter to see through the viewfinder clearly, but when you review the *liquid crystal display* (LCD) screen, you will still need reading glasses to see it. If nearsighted, a plus number is used and you will have to hold the LCD screen close to view the results, because distances will be blurry without corrective lenses.

Some people have difficulty holding the viewfinder next to their eye because their glasses are too thick, ambient light leaks in, or their glasses just aren't strong enough to sharply focus on the image. Here's where diopters are useful. Just like using them on your lens, the same powers of magnification work on the rear of the camera (only the diopters themselves are noticeably smaller).

So how do you determine the diopter size you need? It's more than just a feeling, so consult an optometrist. Tell them your prescription and ask them which size diopter would best work for you. Some people have different eye strengths, so your left eye might use a +3 and your right a +2. If you use the wrong eye, the result will be blurry.

Once you know which strength works for your eye, consult the camera manufacturer and obtain a diopter in the correct strength for your model camera. We've seen prices from $10 to over $50 for a diopter. If you have astigmatism or abnormalities in your eye, a diopter might not work. Others need a combination of diopters to see clearly. Just ask and you will be told if a diopter will work for you. Once you have one, remember to remove your glasses or contacts to sharply see the image. When you have someone else look in the viewfinder, they won't see things as clearly as you, but that could be a good thing. Now nobody will want to borrow your camera. Just don't tell them that the diopter will unscrew.

#51 How to Use Extension Tubes or Bellows

When shooting close-ups with a digital camera that has a removable lens, you have a couple options. You can use a series of rings that form an extension barrel for your camera's close-ups, moving your lens farther from the camera's body. This is called an extension tube. These tubes are a fixed length and cannot be adjusted.

Another option is a bellows extension that will attach directly to the camera body with the lens of your choice mounted on the end in order to provide the amount of magnification preferred. When using a bellows, you can swing or actually angle the lens on the front of the bellows to help adjust your focus and depth of field. The farther away the lens moves from the camera, the greater the magnification. The bellows is flexible, allowing you to extend or compress it to get the shot.

Mount your extension rings or bellows directly to the camera and then select the lens best suited for the shot. Use your camera's LCD display screen or through-the-lens viewfinder to frame your photograph. A carryover from 35mm cameras, these devices have been around for a long time.

Moving the lens farther from the camera also moves the aperture farther away, reducing its size. A camera's built-in through-the-lens exposure meter should adequately compensate. As with all close-up photography, be sure to use a tripod and a cable release, and focus very carefully.

The simplest way to focus is sometimes to move the camera farther away or closer to your subject after you get the proper amount of magnification, much like using a diopter in front of the lens. Neither system, extension tubes nor bellows, takes a "better" shot. Both operate much the same way and it's your choice which to use when shooting. Therefore, having a camera with interchangeable lens does offer a lot more options than a point and shoot camera. Figure 5-8a shows an example of a bellows.

#52 How to Use Backlight

Backlighting is a type of lighting where the strongest portion of the light is coming from behind the subject—whether created by a lighting instrument or naturally from the sun. The backlight mode on the camera compensates for this by opening up the camera's iris slightly to let in more light, overexposing the background (backlit area) slightly, but it properly exposes the subject because he or she would normally be dark or underexposed. Backlight mode and backlighting are different in that backlighting is the "effect" and backlight mode is the way to compensate and correct it. Some people purposely set up a backlight "look" with models because, if done correctly, it looks flattering. Most people just adapt to it by compensating for the effect, but it also may be created. This type of lighting looks great, but it requires some extra care.

Figure 5-8a

Is Dr. Bellows in the house?

The backlight mode on your camera is best used when light is coming from behind your subject, throwing their features into shadow, or when your subject is in the shade, but the background is lit brightly. You must compensate to get a good exposure.

Your camera will have a symbol representing this scenario, but you may need to check your owner's manual to make sure you have the proper setting. The camera will now expose for the subject's features rather than the brighter background. Essentially, the camera is opening up one or two stops, allowing the background to overexpose slightly while normally exposing the subject.

The flash will fire automatically to illuminate or fill in the shadows if it's not compensating by opening the iris. If you take the picture without utilizing this mode, your subject will be lost in the picture as there's no light striking him or her from the front, leaving the person in shadow. This isn't a pleasing picture.

If your camera does not have this shooting mode, you could try using the light coming in through a window and bouncing the light back onto your subject using a large white cloth or piece of cardboard. The key is to have more light falling on the background rather than the subject. Just make sure you compensate and don't expose the background or the effect will be lost.

Figure 5-9 shows a good example of backlighting. With the sun on the subject's back, the exposure is taken from the talent and is set accordingly, allowing the background to glow slightly. The end result is a soft and diffused light. A shot like this evokes a warm, fuzzy feeling.

Figure 5-9

A little backlight goes a long way.

#53 How to Shoot in Limited Light

We all have our limitations and with digital photography, lighting may be the only real limitation. Existing light is considered light that is already present inside a room or outdoors. It may be light being cast by the sun when outdoors or lights or candles when indoors.

Normally, indoor lighting, whether it is incandescent or fluorescent, is sufficient for shooting good digital pictures. Many people, knowing what they can do with the options on their digital camera, avoid using the flash and go with a soft, existing-light shot. Existing light is normally not too direct or harsh, so shadows seldom are an issue.

Using existing light as often as possible tends to make your image very natural looking and flattering. Some of the finest portraits you'll see were accomplished by using existing light and bouncing additional light onto the subject with white cloth or white foam core (white cardboard with a foam core). You can also remove lampshades and open drapes or blinds. Figure 5-10 shows a portrait shot with existing light.

Figure 5-10

Existing light portrait

In the days of 35mm film photography, you had issues that aren't present with a digital camera. The first was grain. The less light in the shot, the bigger and more evident the grain was. The only way to eliminate this problem was to increase the speed of the film, allowing more light and grain. The faster the film (a higher American Standards Association [ASA] or ISO), the lower the light levels needed in which to shoot, but you would be shooting in a grainfest. Digital cameras allow you to change the speed or ISO of the image without the nasty side effect of grain.

Shooting in candlelight at 1600 ISO on a digital camera will deliver a clearly exposed image without any grain (not so with film). When working with a low light level, choose a high ISO speed. Figure 5-11 shows a candlelit birthday party. Notice the lack of grain.

The other inherent problem with film is color temperature. When you shot Junior's third birthday, the images on film were exposed, but very grainy and orange. Candlelight produces an orange light, but not quite as orange as the negative shows. This is because the color temperature is so low on daylight film stock that it reproduces color in the warmer or orange side of the spectrum. A little bit of orange is enchanting, but we don't live in an orange-colored world.

The option that corrects this problem in film is a blue 80A filter that can convert the orange tungsten light to a blue daylight balance. Unfortunately, an 80A filter takes up a few stops of light, something you really don't have in candlelight.

Figure 5-11

Candlelight without the grain

Digital solves this problem by allowing you to change the color balance of the shot. By setting your camera to the indoors or tungsten setting, most of the orange will disappear because the image is no longer exposed for daylight. A little of the orange will remain because candlelight is much lower on the Kelvin scale than pure 3200-degree tungsten, but this is acceptable.

A tripod will probably be required for many of these shots, so always have one nearby. We suggest having two tripods when possible, since they are inexpensive. More expensive fluid head units are better suited for video; you will not need a fluid pan or tilt in still photography. A tripod that's steady is more advantageous. By having two tripods, you can always have one available in your vehicle and another at home or in the studio.

If your camera allows you to switch from automatic to manual, do so and change your sensitivity setting on your camera to its maximum. Using the most sensitive setting on your camera, such as ISO 400 (or higher if your camera is capable), allows you to capture the best picture in limited lighting settings.

If you can adjust your camera's lens opening, use F1.4 or F2, which will allow the most light to be utilized. Be careful when focusing because at these apertures (basically wide open), not as much of your subject will be really sharp because your depth of field (or focus) is extremely narrow. Check the results in your camera as you change your aperture or move around within a given area. Even though the amount of light you have to work with remains unchanged, sometimes the camera position or camera angle may allow more or less ambient light to enter through your lens.

Some of the most appealing outdoor landscape pictures are taken early in the morning or close to sunset, again using the light that Mother Nature has provided. The color temperature here is also much lower and more in the orange spectrum. The images always look better in the picture (more colorful and orange) than they do to the naked eye (or clothed for that matter).

If you're not totally happy with what you visualized when you took your picture, you can always do some tweaking on your computer later. Isn't digital wonderful?

#54 How to Shoot in Bright Sun

Some of the most common and popular types of images are those shot in the bright sunlight. Whether it's skiing, the beach, on just being outside on a sunny day, you know you will have enough light to properly expose the shot.

Many people think that the perfect time for taking pictures of the kids and dogs playing is when the sun is brightly shining. The truth is that with lots of sunlight, the light can become too harsh, especially in the snow or on the beach. One of the drawbacks of the sun is shadows, and most of the time they fall where you don't want them.

Cowboys in western films always seem to have enough light under their hats when in reality if you shot the same thing, the hat would totally shade the subject's face. In Hollywood, lights or reflectors always send light under a cowboy's hat to reduce the shadows.

In bright sunlight, you want your subject to be lit by the sun, but not to the extent that he or she is looking directly into the sun. The last thing you want is your subject squinting because the sun is hitting him or her directly in the face. On the other hand, you don't want to shoot directly into the sun because your exposure will go wild. Keeping the sun at your back, try to find something that will shade your subject slightly without making him or her appear dark.

You'll also want to be careful to avoid positions that cause dark shadows to obscure faces. If possible, try to position subjects so that soft, diffused light off a building or possibly a tree illuminates them.

If you're outside and you see large clouds approaching, wait until the clouds pass in front of the sun to provide softer light for your human subjects. Slightly overcast skies are much better for taking pictures outside because the light is more diffused.

When at the beach or in the snow, avoid taking shots at the brightest part of the day if possible. The shadows are lower early in the morning and late in the afternoon than at high noon. It may be difficult to check your LCD outside in the sun, but if you see sun blaring on your subjects, they will be squinting. Try sunglasses (on them, not you) to eliminate this. Figure 5-12 shows a beach image without any squinting because a four- by four-foot piece of diffusion filtered the sunlight and made the shot more appealing.

#55 How to Photograph the Moon

Since photography has been invented, people have been trying to shoot the moon—unsuccessfully. Why is a tiny white dot in the sky so difficult to shoot? The answer to this could be because it is also giving off light (reflecting it actually) and it makes determining the exposure difficult.

Figure 5-12

A little less sun on the beach

Most cameras have reflected metering systems that measure the amount of light reflected off an object. Instead, you should use an incident meter or one that reads the amount of light falling on an object to get a more accurate exposure.

A photograph of the moon is the type of shot that your digital point and shoot camera won't be able to handle because of the lack of exposure control. That's not to say that with your zoom capabilities maxed to the limit you won't see the moon to some degree—you will. This type of shot requires a large telephoto lens, the camera mounted on a tripod, and a cable release. The location from which you shoot should be totally dark and away from any extraneous light to be most effective. This also makes it difficult to get readings from your camera, but a pocket flashlight will help you. Like the sheriff said, "Get out of town" to avoid pollution, dust, and the scattered city light. Also choose dry weather. Humid nights (even without visible mist) are worse than dry ones and a time when the moon is full (if that's what you want to shoot).

Keep in mind that the moon is a moving target. Because of the earth's rotation, the moon appears to move approximately half its diameter in one minute, so very long exposures are best avoided. The best time to photograph a moonset usually is during a full moon or the day after.

For unusual situations, such as photographing the moon rising above a nearby tall building or setting above a mountain, the best time may be several days before or after the full moon. Without playing around with the image in Photoshop, you can still get a great shot with your digital camera.

The key here is exposure and shutter speed. We prefer a faster shutter speed to avoid movement and blurring. If you take a reading off the moon itself, your image will be underexposed because the moon is reflecting light, but by opening your iris to 2.8, your image will overexpose against a dark sky.

We recommend the longest lens you can find, a 300mm being the minimum. Try setting your shutter speed to 1/500 of a second. This eliminates movement on your part and the moon's. The f-stop should be small, usually F11 or F8. Also, because every situation is slightly different, try bracketing your exposures (have each subsequent image be a half-stop over or under the previous one) and review the results in your LCD.

#56 How to Shoot Fireworks

As much fun as they are to watch, fireworks are equally as challenging to photograph, but not impossible. The kind of camera you use really doesn't matter as long as you have manual controls. Fireworks create a very bright light source, and cameras set for automatic exposures will miss the exposure every time. You really need to use your manual controls to get the best results.

Almost any lens, wide-angle or telephoto, that gives you the desired perspective will work. Because your exposures will usually be around F8 or F11, a fast lens isn't a concern. Some may think because fireworks are dimly illuminated in the night sky that a slow shutter speed and a wide-open iris are the best bet. The exact opposite is true.

Choosing a good viewing position should be one of your first considerations, and try to have something in the photo that's identifiable. It could be a building, bridge, or monument, whatever you can come up with. Having water in the foreground to reflect the fireworks also works well.

Numerous considerations must be made when choosing a location from which to shoot. Find out which way the wind is blowing and try to get upwind. Fireworks create smoke and if the wind is blowing toward your position, it not only blocks the shot, but makes it uncomfortable for you. From the right position, you can use the smoke to your advantage.

As the fireworks build, the smoke reflects light, which can help define the shot. Research beforehand and look for a unique position from which to shoot. It's not always easy to get approval to shoot from an unusual location, but the results will be worth the effort. Most photographers recommend using a slower film speed, such as ISO 100 or 64, and shoot slide film. Some photographers shoot daylight-balanced film, while others shoot tungsten film. It's a matter of personal preference. Still others prefer color negative film because it has greater exposure latitude and contrast control. Your digital camera set in automatic mode can compensate for color temperature, or if you prefer a specific temperature, adjust it manually to tungsten or daylight.

Keep in mind, it's basically impossible to predict how a series of fireworks will look, and a certain amount of luck is involved. You never know how good the burst will be, so shoot, bracket your exposures, and check your images (time permitting) to see where you're getting the best results. We've found that the longer the fireworks display goes, the better they get, so don't be frustrated by those you may have missed early on. Be ready for the finale.

#57 How to Take Time Exposures

Most people seem to shy away from doing time exposures because they think they are difficult and not worth the effort. On the contrary, certain kinds of shots can only be made when the shutter is open for an extended period of time and they are all more than worth the effort.

To do a time exposure, digital cameras will have a T for time or a B for the bulb setting. In this mode, the shutter will stay open as long as you press the shutter release or, on some models, until you press the shutter release a second time to close it.

A tripod is mandatory for shooting a time exposure because any movement will blur and ruin the image. Pressing down on the shutter release will move the camera if it isn't fastened securely to a tripod. Cable releases offer freedom from jarring the camera and allow you to keep the shutter open for extended periods of time.

How long should you keep the shutter open for a time exposure? That's a good question with a hundred different answers. Our best response is "depending on what you want to shoot," but usually less is more. Let's look at a few examples and see how long the shutter is opened for each. The first is a short time exposure of a waterfall.

If you want the waterfall to have a different kind of look, try shooting it in a time exposure rather than at an extremely fast shutter speed. A normal shot of flowing water freezes the action because the shutter speed is 1/250 or 1/500 of a second or faster. Almost all images of waterfalls are shot this way. But by shooting it with a time exposure, the water now becomes a silk-like formation that looks as if it were painted. Since the shutter is opened for a longer period of time, the water continues to move as the CCD is exposing the image, resulting in a blurred motion, much like you get when someone moves quickly on camera with a slow shutter speed.

Figure 5-13 shows a waterfall shot with a three-second exposure. The shutter remained open for three full seconds, allowing a lot of movement to occur. Once again, to increase the depth of field when shooting a waterfall, shoot at the smallest aperture your lens will allow. In our case, this was F22.

Take an exposure reading and determine what the shutter speed should be. In our example, since we shot at dusk, the shutter speed was 1/15 of a second, still too fast to blur the movement of the water. Using a tripod and an ND9 filter (chewing up three stops of light), we were getting closer to the three-second mark, but not close enough. If we kept the shutter open for three seconds now, we would have blurred movement but also ended up with an overexposed image. Instead we waited another half-hour until the ambient light got dark enough to make a three-second exposure correct and then we took the picture.

Our next example is a house shot at night with the only illumination being a street lamp and the interior lights of the home. Once again, try

Figure 5-13

A time exposure of a waterfall

Figure 5-14

A house at night with a time exposure

an exposure and view the results on your LCD screen until you achieve the desired effect with the exposure time. It took us three tries before we got the result shown in Figure 5-14. This is where digital really shines. Instead of waiting until the film gets processed and noticing you are over- or underexposed, you see the results immediately. Most have a tendency to overexpose the image by leaving the shutter open too long. Our house example was eight seconds. If you could see this image in color you would notice how the different color temperatures of the lights created various hues in the windows and the streetlight.

The last example may be the one you are most familiar with: traffic patterns at night. By shooting cars in a time exposure, the trail of white headlights and red taillights creates an interesting pattern. Fast movement won't register and slow movement will create a brighter image.

Try this type of shot yourself. The longer you open your iris, the more defined the lines will be in the final picture as if someone had painted the road with light. *National Geographic* has been shooting these types of shots for decades. Experiment with different settings and use the one you like most. That's what digital is for, because you can see the results.

Chapter 6

Using the Modes

#58 How to Use Your Camera in Different Mode Settings

Digital cameras have lots of different mode settings that allow you to choose which type of shot you'd like to take. This chapter examines different types of modes such as automatic and manual mode, preferred and priority mode, backlight mode, portrait and landscape mode, beach and snow mode, sunset mode, and macro mode.

#59 How to Use the Camera in Automatic Mode

The easiest way to shoot anything is to have the camera set in automatic mode. Digital units are sophisticated enough to determine the correct shutter speed, aperture setting, and focus. This automatic mode takes most of the guesswork out of shooting, allowing you more freedom to compose the picture, but most professionals and serious amateurs would rather set everything themselves than use the automatic mode.

The camera is not foolproof and times will occur when it tells you something, and you know a better way of doing it. When you take readings before you shoot, look at the f-stop and shutter speed. Do they make sense or could something in the shot be throwing them off?

Your digital camera probably has an automatic exposure mode that sets the exposure for you. You'll still need to make sure the camera knows exactly what you want to base your exposure on. In other words, what is the main subject of your picture? Point your camera at that and let it determine the correct f-stop and shutter speed. If the reading doesn't make sense and is too light or dark, try taking another reading, this time closer to the subject. Sometimes unwanted reflections or ambient light may be the culprit.

When we get a new camera, we always test the camera's exposure against a light meter. We use both the exposure and the light meter in the reflected setting because few cameras take incident readings. If the camera's exposure is different than the light meter, which should you trust? The light meter is calibrated and the camera averages all the light levels striking the *charge-coupled device* (CCD). This is why you should rely on the *liquid crystal display* (LCD) monitor on the camera. If the image looks too dark or light, adjust the exposure by half a stop and then up to a full stop.

Compose your picture as you normally would and check whether you have any very dark or very bright areas that could possibly fool the meter in your camera. It's easier to do than you may think. If your picture area contains either of these dark or light areas, move in closer and reframe so that only the area you want exposed is seen in the viewfinder.

By pressing your shutter button halfway down and holding it there, the camera will lock in the exposure. Move back to your original position, reframe, and take your picture by holding the shutter release button all the way down.

Automatic exposure is the best setting to use if you need to take a picture quickly and don't have time to determine all the settings manually. Of course, you should never be rushed when taking a picture, but sometimes you may not be in control of the situation, such as if you spotted Elvis (this would be a good time to use the automatic mode).

#60 How to Use the Camera in Manual Mode

If you'd like to do all the camera settings yourself, does that make you more professional? Not necessarily. Automatic features have come a long way, but sometimes the manual mode is what's needed when capturing that illusive image.

The majority of the time, you can feel comfortable with setting your camera to automatic and just shooting. The digital cameras on the market do a good job of determining the exposure automatically, but they really don't know what you want the exposure set for. Some of the most sophisticated models have meters that examine different parts of the picture area and determine the best overall proper exposure. With five or more metering "zones," the camera has a pretty good idea of the exposure. If your camera has a manual mode, you should definitely experiment with it, as it can help you when shooting in challenging settings and also give you some creative flexibility.

If you're taking pictures outside on a sunny day with snow covering the ground, the camera may be fooled by what it determines to be a lot of light or brightness, and your images might end up looking darker than what you'd like. Figure 6-1 shows how the camera sees the subject with snow covering the ground. In this instance, too much white was present for the meter to properly expose the image.

In manual mode, you'll want to adjust your aperture or shutter speed when excessive brightness (sand or snow) or darkness (a dark building or a mound of coal) would fool the camera's meter. Why you might want to take someone's picture in a mound of coal is your business.

First, take a reading of the subject in the snow. Then take another reading of a close-up of his or her face and note the difference in the readings. Usually, the camera's lens will need to be opened by two stops. By opening your iris two stops, a person may be normally exposed in the snow. Of course, the snow now will be overexposed by two stops, but it just makes the snow look that much cleaner. Figure 6-2 shows a properly exposed image in the snow because the camera was set on manual and a reading was taken of the subject's face.

This is where it is critical to open up (use a larger f-stop) or close down (you guessed it—use a lower f-stop) and review your images in

#60

Figure 6-1

My, how dark you look in the snow.

Figure 6-2

Isn't this a better image
(unless you have to shovel all
the snow)?

the camera. Using a digital camera effectively in manual mode to be
more creative is something that will come with time and experience.

#61 How to Use the Camera in Preferred
or Priority Mode

Higher-end digital cameras have settings called *preferred* or *priority*
mode. These modes allow you to specifically choose how you want
your camera set with a specific function to be controlled.

Naturally, you'll want to take advantage of all the selection modes
that your camera has to offer. They vary from one manufacturer to
another, but most cameras have settings to program how you prefer to
have your pictures exposed.

One of Nikon's point and shoot models has quite a few selections.
For example, *auto mode* is used for snapshots and is recommended for
photos that may later be retouched on a computer. Everything is controlled for you and the camera senses which f-stop, shutter speed, and
exposure mode to use.

Party/indoor mode is used for shots where low light conditions may
exist. This normally switches the color balance to tungsten to remove
some of the orange from the shot. A tripod is useful but not essential
because you may need to support the camera to avoid movement during the exposure.

#62 How to Use the Camera in Backlight Mode

Backlight mode is used when light is coming from behind your subject, causing shadows and underexposures. Without selecting this feature, the camera's automatic exposure is reading the brightest thing in the picture, the background, and exposing for it.

If someone is standing in front of a window indoors, the background is brighter and the backlight setting is necessary because the person is being lit from the back. Figure 6-3 shows an image that was captured without using the backlight mode setting. The situation is corrected in Figure 6-4. In this mode, the flash will fire automatically to fill in the shadows.

#63 How to Use the Camera in Portrait Mode

Portrait mode is used when the main subject needs to stand out clearly and you want the background details to be softened or blurred, giving a sense of depth. The degree to which background details are softened depends upon the amount of light available.

Figure 6-3

A person being lit by backlight mode and the camera has not corrected for it.

Figure 6-4

Backlight mode used correctly, a more pleasing picture

#65

#64 How to Use the Camera in Landscape Mode

Landscape mode is used for vivid landscape photos that enhance the colors and contrasts in the subjects, such as forests and landscapes. The electronic circuits in the camera function to enhance the colors.

#65 How to Shoot in Landscape Mode

Shooting in landscape mode allows you to capture the beauty and majesty of a wide, sweeping vista. With the format of the image being wider than tall, the landscape mode lends itself to . . . landscapes.

The landscape mode on most digital cameras is identified by a symbol that closely depicts an overall landscape view. This mode enhances outlines, colors, and contrasts in subjects such as skyscapes and forests. Simply adjust your camera to this mode and take your picture.

Of course, you can take other types of pictures while in landscape mode, but they should be ones that a horizontal format would accentuate. Portraits, on the other hand, demand a closer, more vertical format and are not suited for landscape mode. Images taken of the desert, mountain ranges, sunsets with sailboats dotting the horizon, ski slopes with powdery snow capping the trees, and lush gardens populated with a myriad of colorful flowers are perfect to photograph using a wider f-ormat.

Hollywood establishes the first shot of every movie they make this way. The term *establishing shot* is the name given to this wide style because it establishes the setting where the action will take place. You can do the same thing with your digital camera: Establish the location with a wide landscape shot and then move in closer for the people or portrait shots.

Thus, the word landscape is often described as a horizontal shot, as opposed to a portrait or vertical shot. But as with anything, rules are made to be broken. For example, if you were to photograph an extremely tall building, a vertically held camera in landscape mode is the way to go. It all depends on your subject.

#66 How to Use the Camera in Beach or Snow Mode

Beach or snow mode captures the brightness of snowy fields, beaches, or the sun going down over large bodies of water. Exactly the opposite of backlight, this setting closes the iris slightly for an exposure.

#67 How to Use the Camera in Sunset Mode

Sunset mode captures the beautiful reds in sunrises or sunsets exactly as you see them, instead of the camera accentuating them. The expo-sure also compensates for the bright sky against dark clouds by aver-aging the exposure so both are pleasingly balanced.

#68 How to Use the Camera in Macro Mode

Macro mode lets you focus the camera within inches of the subject. If you wanted to shoot something farther away, the camera would not focus while in macro. For us, macro means magnify. The next solution discusses this more explicitly.

Priority mode allows you to emphasize one object in the scene over something else. The aperture's priority or preferred mode sets the f-stop first and then sets the shutter speed accordingly, while the opposite is true if the shutter speed has the priority.

Different manufacturers call each of these settings by different names. Some just have icons that allow you to select the mode you prefer, whereas others give you more choices, helping you determine exactly what you want to control (besides yourself).

#69 How to Shoot Macro Images

If you want to get very up close and personal with your subject in digital photography, then macro is the way to go. Macro allows you to make an extreme close-up and still be able to focus sharply.

If you'll be doing a lot of close-ups or tabletop shooting and haven't made a final decision on which digital camera to purchase, be sure the cameras you're considering have a close-up (macro) setting. Otherwise, you'll be limited to the close-up capabilities that come with the camera, which could be as far as three feet away.

High-quality LCD displays or through-the-lens optical viewing (with a single-lens reflex model) allow you to shoot close-ups much easier. Keep in mind that lower-cost digital cameras with fixed-focus lenses may not have any focusing capabilities at all, so a macro shot will be out of the question.

Figure 6-5 illustrates a butterfly that was shot in macro. We could have accomplished the same thing with a telephoto lens, but we desired the slight magnification that a close-up or macro lens allows.

Cameras in the past offered a *micro* focusing capability. Different than macro, a micro lens can get you close to the subject (like a microscope) but offers no magnification, allowing more distortion in the image.

Other cameras have macro capabilities but are not true macro lenses. If your camera has interchangeable lenses, then you can purchase a true macro that will get you close to your subject. Macros that are included on a zoom lens have a "macro range," but they aren't true macro lenses because they have to function as a regular lens and only occasionally in macro mode.

Depending on the camera, you can shoot close-ups with a macro lens, a bellows extension, or an extension ring, all of which should give you adequate magnification. You'll definitely need a sturdy tripod and a

Figure 6-5

A butterfly shot
in macro mode

cable release for these types of shots. It can also be difficult to light your subject, depending on how much distance is between the lens and your subject. A built-in flash on your camera will probably be too harsh in such close proximity to the object.

Often the best way to light your subject is to bounce light onto a white card or sheet. This softer approach won't melt anything in front of the lens. If you have lighting other than a flash, such as tungsten lights, you can try skimming light across the surface of your subject to get the most detail.

In order to get the most depth of field, be sure to shoot at the smallest f-stop possible. Focus is also critical in macro mode, where a 1/4-inch distance from the subject may be blurry. Sometimes just moving slightly closer or farther away from the subject may aid in macro focusing.

If magnification is what you're after, try shooting in macro. Figure 6-6 shows another butterfly shot with a telephoto lens, but note that something is lacking from the image. Getting extremely close with a macro produces a better image with less flattening (compression) and more flattering imagery than a telephoto shot.

Figure 6-6

A butterfly shot with a telephoto lens

There you have it. The choice is yours depending on the "look" you desire. If you want magnification—go with a macrolens (macro-magnify). If you prefer a close-up without the magnification—use a telephoto lens. The subject will be sharp and the background blurred.

Chapter 7

How to Compose Your Images

#70 How to Compose Your Images

Composition is the key to making your digital images look professional. In this chapter, you'll learn how to frame a shot, work with depth of field, and work with foregrounds and backgrounds. You'll also learn to shoot objects entering or leaving the frame, judge distances, avoid distortion, and use auto-focus effectively.

#71 How to Frame a Shot

This is one of the best times in life to be framed. When looking through the viewfinder, you want to tell a story with what's in the frame and make it look nice in the process.

When thinking about or composing your picture, you can do a number of things to make your final image more interesting. Look for shapes of any kind that can create a frame effect around your main subject. Try shooting through a doorway, window, tree branches, or an archway. These are the most obvious frames you can create, but many more exist.

You may ultimately change the location of where you first thought about taking your picture and end up with a totally different look. You might find yourself shooting through a large piece of pipe, a staircase, or even through a wall with bricks missing.

Be sure to frame your foreground rather than the background. You want something that appears in front of your subject just as an actual frame would. Because we live in a three-dimensional world, our photos should have "depth" with objects being on different planes. By creating a frame this way, you can instantly give your picture a three-dimensional look. This brings up another point: weight. Having something too large or heavy off to the far right of left of the frame throws off the balance or weight of the image.

Centering is important for this kind of balance. Just by looking at some pictures you can tell when the weight or balance is off and it just doesn't look right. Figure 7-1 shows an improperly balanced or weighted picture. Figure 7-2 corrects the problem by centering the subject to balance the image.

Figure 7-1

It ain't heavy. It's just an unbalanced picture.

Figure 7-2

Happiness is a balanced picture.

You can either have your frame in focus (sharp) or slightly out of focus if you think that including it will detract from the picture. If you decide you want to take a nice picture of your house and you feel it needs something interesting as a frame, try taking a small piece of branch from a nearby tree and placing it at the edge of the frame. If you're shooting with a tripod, look through the viewfinder and place the branch where it adds to the picture and make your exposure. If you find yourself without a tripod, see if someone can hold the branch close to the lens where it's most effective. Frame the picture and review your image to see if it's what you want. Figure 7-3 shows how a branch can give depth to a shot by making the framing more appealing. Figure 7-4 shows how trees can be used to frame a flag, making a great picture.

#72 How to Work with Depth of Field

The term *depth of field* is controllable and determines how much depth or distance in your image is in sharp focus. Two things largely decide how deep your depth of field will be: the f-stop and the lens' focal length.

Depth of field is a powerful composition tool used to focus attention on a certain part of your subject and to help eliminate a distracting background. If you have both manual focus and exposure controls with your camera, you'll have a greater reign over depth of field, but any digital camera can use this tool.

Figure 7-3

A branch of a tree to make an appealing image

Figure 7-4

A flag framed with trees

#72

With a single-lens reflex camera, you can preview your image with your depth of field preview button. The depth of field preview button will stop the lens down to the aperture you want to use and enable you to view what will be in focus and what will not be, thus making it a useful tool.

As mentioned earlier, the depth of field depends on the size of the lens opening, the distance from your subject, and the focal length of the lens. Use the smallest lens opening you can to get the most depth of field in your picture. The smaller apertures such as F16 or F22 will give you more depth of field than a larger aperture of F2.8 or F2.0. Your wide-angle lenses will also have more depth of field at a particular f-stop than a telephoto lens. Depth of field can draw attention to your subject and subdue the background to the extent that the background may not be recognizable. That's why this is something that should be controlled by you, the photographer.

Wider shots with wide-angle lenses are usually landscape or group shots. Here you need everything in sharp focus, but if you want to call attention to something specific in a frame, blurring the background with a telephoto lens and a wider aperture is the method to use.

Figure 7-5 shows a flower shot with a normal lens at F16. Figure 7-6 is more appealing because the background is softer and diffused. Your eye goes directly to the flower you want everyone to see. Shot at the same f-stop, this image used a telephoto lens to blur the background.

Figure 7-5

Which flower do you want the viewer to notice?

Figure 7-6

No doubt exists as to which flower is the attention grabber.

#73 How to Photograph Foregrounds

Depending on the type of picture you're taking, the foreground can be a very important area of concern. When shooting children, you can include the favorite blanket Grandma made or some books, toys, and games. The eye is drawn to the foreground and if you can do some obvious things to eliminate a distraction or add to the overall shot, take the time to do so.

This could be as simple as getting closer to your subject or using a telephoto or zoom lens. You might consider changing camera angles or heights. In many situations, you can use your depth of field to emphasize a foreground object. If your digital camera has the option to change its aperture, open up by using a smaller numbered f-stop, such as F2 or F2.8.

If a business owner asks you to take a picture of his or her building, think about the best time of day to take the shot. Obviously, it would be nice to have some sunlight striking the front or entrance, but more importantly ask yourself, "Could this shot be done before or after normal business hours?" If the business is closed over the weekend, consider shooting then. This way you'll eliminate customers entering and leaving the building, and most importantly you probably won't have any vehicles parked in front of the building that could hide important facets.

The biggest obstacle in taking a good exterior building photo is to avoid having any vehicles identifiable in the foreground that would date the picture. Building exteriors don't change their appearance often. It's not necessary to tell anyone when the picture was taken.

In some cases, you're simply going to have to deal with the foreground while taking the shot and make any necessary changes electronically later with your software program (removing telephone poles, wires, and so on). Anything you can do before pressing the shutter release button on your digital camera will save you time on the computer after the shot.

#74 How to Use Backgrounds

Most people tend to focus (a camera term) on the subject in front of the camera, often not thinking about what is behind the object. This may be a purchased or borrowed roll of background paper (often referred to as seamless), a neatly draped canvas (sometimes called muslin), or a painted image or photograph.

A background can be a plus or a minus, so it's important to determine how it will affect your finished picture before you take your first shot. One way of determining how your background will look on camera is to simply grab a shot and review it in the camera before placing your subject in place. How does the light strike the surface? Do you need a kicker light on the subject to separate him or her from the background?

Be sure to check your background to make sure it's not too bright or dark, too distracting or annoying because it's too busy, or more interesting than your subject. If a splotch of paint catches your eye more than Wanda Lou in her prom dress, you may need to focus more on the subject (there's that focus word again).

When shooting portraits, you can use a seamless background and, by using additional lights directed toward the background, create subtle colors or shadows to highlight or contrast with it. A background with the cloth or material arranged in a creative way can also be effective. If you are on location and don't have access to a seamless or canvas, an executive office may also be an effective background depending on how the picture is to be used.

When shooting outdoors, choose an interesting but not overpowering background. A deep blue sky with a few clouds will add interest to any scenic shot you may take. If the sky isn't quite the way you'd like to see it, you are still in control of the situation. Take the picture and work your magic at home with your various software tools (more information on this will be discussed in future chapters). Try to be aware of any trees, poles, shrubs, or other objects directly behind the head of your subject. You don't want the subject to appear as though something is growing out of his or her head. Everyone has seen these pictures and laughed after the fact, that is, everyone except the photographer who didn't notice it when the image was taken.

Curved or straight lines can be good for your compositions, but don't allow them to become distracting. If the background is going to take away from the picture or be distracting, consider using your depth of field to blur as much of the background as possible. Figure 7-7 illustrates how this technique adds to the picture.

#75 How to Work with Objects Entering the Frame

Whenever you photograph an object that is moving or pointed in a certain direction, always have that object coming *into* the frame.

Figure 7-7

Nice background! Too bad the subject in the foreground wasn't more interesting.

#75

Regardless of whether the subject is an animal, automobile, tractor, or train, consider that they all have a front and a back (like most people too).

These objects or subjects should be facing toward the camera or at least looking into the frame. If your object or subject is looking or heading out of the frame, the viewer will tend to want to know what the attraction is out there beyond what they're seeing that is distracting. Your goal is to have the viewer being interested in your subject.

You want the viewer's eye to be drawn to your image area. If you give them other distractions, he or she may look there instead. The viewer shouldn't have to wonder who or what this person is running from or where the train is going. You have a reason for taking the picture, and you need to get the viewer to admire the image and not be thinking about what he or she might not be seeing.

When shooting a fast-moving object, allow for some blank space in front of the object. This gives the impression that the object has somewhere to go, but not to the point of being a distraction. This is also called "leading the image." By having space in front of the person or object, you are essentially leading it into the shot. Give them the space they need.

#76 How to Work with Objects Leaving the Frame

The opposite of the previous solution, when you look at an image and the main subject matter is leaving the frame of the picture, it makes the viewer wonder what is beyond the frame. Is there something interesting that the animal in the picture may want to visit? Is the speedboat about to cross the finish line or the plane about to land?

You may want to intentionally take your picture this way for a given reason; however, most people prefer to show the entire picture to eliminate any questions or doubts. Obviously, if your intention is to capture a car leaving the starting line at your local drag strip, you'll want to shoot from behind the car to see the smoking tires and the car veering off to the side. Objects leaving the frame are not wrong or inappropriate.

Typically, something entering the frame is more common and more interesting, but it's certainly not the only way to take your picture. You can always rotate your image using your photo editor, but don't expect your rotate tool to turn the car around. That's *magic*, not digital photography.

#77 How to Judge Distance

When you take a picture of someone, how far should you be away from him or her? Selecting the distance from where you want to take your picture is an important consideration.

The farther from someone you shoot, the more distant and less personal the viewer feels. Getting very close and seeing the subject's eyes clearly allows you to better identify with him or her. Attractive people are always shot up close because the photographer wants to accentuate the fact that the subject is pleasing to the eye. If done at a distance, no one can tell.

When shooting young children, give them as much space as possible. They have no idea what to expect when having their picture taken. Even though they are the cutest creatures on the planet (just ask their parents), avoid getting too close; instead, have the lens do that for you.

Most digital cameras have zoom capabilities, but that may not help to fill your frame from a great distance away, such as a landscape shot. Normally, try to take a minute and choose your best distance or vantage point. Obviously, you don't want to be too close to your subject and end up having to use a wide-angle lens that could distort the shot.

Our goal is not to give the impression that a building is about to collapse or fall over by the fact we are using a wide angle lens. By getting too close, you risk having this type of look or line convergence.

When photographing a group of people or a single person, move in as close as possible without giving the impression you're in people's faces with the camera. Getting closer allows you to show greater detail and textures that can't be seen at greater distances, and it allows the person's eyes to be shown.

A medium or short telephoto lens can best get you close to your subject and still provide space between the person and your lens. If doing portraits, this medium or slightly telephoto lens is often called a portrait lens (somewhere around 100mm).

If, in your final picture, dead or open space exists at the top, bottom, left, or right of the frame, it should be done on purpose. In other words, this space should add to the overall appearance of your picture. This is where composition is so important. If you don't compose the image correctly, you are sending the wrong message.

By keeping your distance from a subject such as a building, monument, or other stationary subject, you're doing several things. One is you can provide a feeling of depth and space. The sky may add both color and dimension to your picture, and the foreground becomes prominent, which can give the feeling of space or depth. Believe it or not, you are still in control of your images and you need to send the message you want to send.

If you're taking a head and shoulders type shot, you're going to want to fill the frame with your subject and keep the background (what little there is) clean and not distracting. Look at the image you've just shot and make sure you're not too close or that you accidentally crop into the hair or chin.

The larger the image in your camera, the sharper the pictures will be because less enlargement is required. As always, shoot several positions and vary the expressions and head tilts. Of course, be sure to show them to your subject for their approval or suggestions. Delete any images that you would never consider using and keep shooting until everyone is satisfied or exhausted, whichever comes first!

#78 How to Avoid Distortion

The vocabulary work for today is *distortion*. Although not *Webster's* definition, distortion means twisting or changing what is normal. For the most part, any distortion in a picture is annoying.

That's not to say you can't be creative with distorting images, but for now, let's talk about ways to avoid or minimize distortion. The majority of distortion is visible when using telephoto and wide-angle lenses. When shooting with a telephoto lens, if you have several subjects in a row from front to back, the distance between the subjects appears to be compressed. You might be shooting a statue that may be 100 feet in front of the building, but with your telephoto lens the statue will appear to be almost touching or attached to the building. You can minimize this by changing the angle from where you originally intended to shoot. Take a minute and review the image in the camera and determine if a change in position would be helpful. If the objects that you're shooting can be arranged, simply move them farther apart before taking the picture. Usually if you shoot off axis slightly, or not straight ahead, you'll alleviate some of the distortion.

Wide-angle lenses can cause distortion by having the camera too close to the subject. Facial distortion happens frequently when using a wide-angle lens. The nose, forehead, and chin will all appear out of proportion by having the camera too close to your subject. This is often used for a humorous approach, making the subject look silly.

In the same manner, if you use a wide-angle lens and shoot down on someone (not talk down, shoot down), their head appears large and massive in the frame and their feet are a tiny pinpoint. This is because their face is closest to the lens and is distorted from the wide angle. Figure 7-8 illustrates a girl with a big head and tiny feet.

Figure 7-8

My, what a large head of hair you have.

Figure 7-9

Notice how a tilted camera changes one's view of the world.

#78

Taking self-portraits with a wide-angle lens may produce the same effect. When setting the camera on a timer and holding it at arm's length, a wide lens will enlarge the subject in the shot. Unless you desire being called "big head," don't use this type of lens up close and personal.

Use a normal lens for this type of shot if possible, or move away from your subject, which should eliminate the distortion. To avoid any distortion when shooting a building, make sure that your camera is parallel to the building. If the camera is tilted or shot in a Dutch Tilt angle, the building will have the appearance that it's leaning and about to fall down (except the one in Pisa that always looks that way). Review your image until you're comfortable that the building is exactly the way you see it without looking through the camera. If you see distortion through the lens, the camera will see it also. Figure 7-9 shows a tipsy building.

By using an image editor such as Photoshop, you can intentionally distort an image as we mentioned earlier. With different distortion filters, you can turn, twist, twirl, create waves, or make ripples to your image. These images can be definite attention-getters and allow you to be as creative as you want.

Chapter 8

Capturing the Image

#79 How to Capture an Image

With digital cameras, the image is captured or recorded onto a storage medium. This chapter discusses the various ways an image may be captured, including how to control the speed or ISO, how big a file should be, how to shoot in the raw format, how JPEGs and GIFs differ, how to correctly size your image, and how to control brightness and contrast.

#80 How to Control Speed (ISO)

Both digital and 35mm cameras' pictures are controlled by the ISO or film speed. Back in the 1970s, the term for film speed was ASA and was given a rating between 25 to 400. The higher the number, the faster the film or the less light it needs to expose an image. Today the same numbers are referred to as ISO and they can go as high (or fast) as 1,600.

Unfortunately, not all digital cameras allow you to change your ISO, which in digital is a rating system used to compare the speed of the camera's sensors. It's much easier to capture action shots such as sporting events if you can change your ISO to a higher number.

By controlling the ISO, you can shoot pictures in low light using a higher ISO rating, and use a much lower ISO for bright sunlight or snow shots. For the most part, you're going to want to stop the action so your subject can be seen more clearly. Blurred or out of focus pictures showing movement is different and creative, but most times you'll want to get a good look at your subject.

If you can change your camera ISO speed, use its highest setting, which is typically ISO 400 or more. By using a higher ISO, you can use faster shutter speeds without sacrificing depth of field or sharpness. Grain, inherent in older film stocks with high ASA ratings, is no longer a problem. Virtually, no grain exists at 400 ISO, so anything less than that will still be crystal clear. Kodak's MAX film has a speed of 800 ISO, but at lower light levels the grain is visible.

If your camera has a program setting such as *Action*, be sure to set your camera at that setting. The *Action* program mode automatically calculates the best exposure using a higher shutter speed. The camera's computer senses what is best and adjusts the ISO for you.

When taking portraits under a lighting setup in the studio, we usually adjust our ISO to the slowest setting, 100, to get the best images possible. When taking action shots at a sporting event under lower light, 400 ISO is usually the choice. Figure 8-1 illustrates an image shot at

#80

Figure 8-1

Clear, sharp images are recorded at 100 ISO.

Figure 8-2

At 800 ISO, grain is present.

100 ISO. Notice the slight graininess under low light in Figure 8-2 shot at 800 ISO. Take a few seconds to review your images to make sure you're stopping the action and getting nice, sharp pictures.

#81 How Big Should a File Be?

In years past, the question used to be, "How much film do I have left?" Since we are now in the digital era and film isn't an issue, we are more concerned with how much memory we have left (a question we ask ourselves often). The larger the image, the more space it's going to take up on your memory device.

The size of the file will and should vary, depending on how you intend to use the image. Are you planning to e-mail the image to friends and family so that a smaller file size would be sufficient? Is this something special that is intended for publication or must be high quality, requiring a larger size from which to work? You'll need to determine what the file size should be for the end product. Ask yourself, "How am I going to use this picture?" Once you answer that, you will have a better understanding of how large or small the captured image should be. It's certainly to your advantage to avoid having a large file if you don't need one; all it will do is take up valuable space and take a longer time to open. Obviously, the larger file you capture and save, the fewer images you'll be able to record before you need to transfer them from the camera.

If you're shooting the image for yourself, it's your call. You have the option of shooting a file in a larger size and then saving it to another medium in a smaller format. If you are unsure of the image's end usage, shoot the photo in a larger file and archive it much smaller. The quality will still be maintained.

When someone asks you so shoot some pictures of his grandkids because he wants to e-mail them to family, you will be tempted to shoot at a small file size. When Grandpa sees the digital images on your *liquid crystal display* (LCD), he will want some 11 × 16's of everything. Therefore, we always shoot larger and then compress. It's nearly impossible to do it the other way around. If we shot those same potential e-mail images in a lower resolution or file size, enlarging them will bring out all the pixels and imperfections in the shot. In short, always go from larger to smaller, never smaller to larger.

If someone requests that you do some photography for him or her, the person should make the final determination as to the size of the file (providing the person knows what he or she is talking about). When we asked Grandpa, he said he didn't care. Once again, it all falls back on you.

#82 How to Shoot in Raw Format

Although the term "Raw" sounds nasty, digital camera users are excited to have the option available to them. When you discuss an image in a Raw format, you're basically talking about an image that's been captured by your camera and saved onto your memory card. This image is an original and nothing has been done to alter it in any way.

Your camera will give you options on how to save the image film, usually by size. As an example, a Canon D60 offers Raw, Small JPEG, Medium JPEG, and Large JPEG. The Canon also gives you the option of saving the images as TIFF files, but the JPEG's three sizes cover most of the images we take.

As mentioned in a previous solution, the larger the file size, the more space it will take up on your storage device. But with small, medium, and large available as image sizes, why would anyone want to shoot in the Raw format?

Switch your camera to the Raw format and notice how many *megabytes* (MB) your image takes up. On the Canon D60, the Raw format takes up 63MB per image. Having a massive memory card of 512MB, we get less than 10 images saved, more than the 3.2MB the large JPEG file uses (2 small JPEG images can fit on a 1.44 floppy disk). So if you have the option of less than 10 images before clearing the memory or almost 150, which would you choose?

Actually, it's not quite that simple. You need to ask yourself what you intend to do with the image. If you just shoot it, store it, or give it to a friend, you may never use the Raw setting. When shooting and immediately printing the image with no intensions of manipulating the photo, Raw is not the setting to use.

An important word was used in the last paragraph: *manipulating*. If you intend to change the picture in any way (size, color, and so on), Raw is the best format to use. The image is in its purest form: no frills, no compression, no nothing.

If we chose one of the other JPEG settings, the picture would already be compressed. Every time you open, save, and close a JPEG, you are compressing it further. This may not be noticeable after a few openings and closings, but the image is degrading. The Raw file is clean, so opening, changing the hue, removing imperfections, and resizing it will not compress the image at all. Once all the changes have been made, the Raw file can be saved back to JPEG or any other medium.

We take most of our images into Photoshop to tweak them. If an JPEG image is opened, adjusted, saved, closed, opened again to be reviewed, saved, closed, and opened again to be printed, we've already compressed the Wazoo out of it. Once the client has accepted the Raw file, it is then converted into JPEG for printing. The size of the RAW file makes it difficult to download or even print. The original RAW image can be saved on a CD, hard drive, or erased if you are sure it's no longer needed (that never happens).

On a recent legal shoot, we had to take over 80 images of a patient's injuries. On the 512MB disk we saved the images to, we would have had plenty of room if we had shot everything in large JPEGs. But each image had to be reviewed by the client, enlarged, touched up, shaded, and many other things before the judicial system got their hands on them. Obviously, this would have been a nightmare with 80 JPEGS. The client only ended up choosing 11 from the 80, but we still shot all images in Raw format, filling many memory cards in the process.

Each image was selected, retouched, and saved as a JPEG for printing. The remaining 69 Raw files were saved onto five CD-ROMs and archived. This process takes up more space, but when you know you will be editing the pictures, Raw is the only way to travel.

Using a Raw file is much like going back to a film camera's negative. This is the best source from which to make changes. If we did the same thing from a 4 × 6 print, we'd have to reshoot the photograph again and work with the new negative or Raw file (but it still is one generation down from the original).

Once you've captured the Raw image, you then use your photo image editor to enhance and save the image to whatever format you wish. Aren't you glad you know what Raw can do for you now? Somehow it doesn't sound quite as nasty.

#83 What Is a GIF?

Both JPEGs and GIFs are formats for digital photos. Each has their own strengths and weaknesses, so one format may be better than another in a particular instance. This section will educate you on just two of the many different types of photo files.

Let's begin with a GIF. To begin with, a GIF is a much smaller file format than a JPEG, meaning it takes up less space in your storage medium. That could be considered the good news. As for the bad, a GIF will only give you 256 colors in your image. That may sound like quite a lot, but with millions of colors available in the spectrum, this is just a small part of the pie.

The colors used in a GIF file are also very flat and not as vibrant as other files' colors. This could be because only 256 get to come out and play. When sending a digital image to someone via e-mail, a GIF will take a lot less time to upload and download. But, once again, a problem occurs. Larger files could be progressively downloaded so that you can see an image gradually appear on your screen; a GIF cannot be progressively built.

Logos are great to send as Christmas GIFs (sorry) because of the smaller size file and the smaller amount of colors, as well as the fact that flat color works better with these. Adobe Photoshop gives you the option of saving in GIF, but only do so if you don't mind living with the results.

A lot of web sites use GIF images because they take up less real estate on a web page. However, smaller thumbnail images are still usually JPEGs.

#84 What Is a JPEG?

A JPEG is mostly the opposite of a GIF. Being a much larger file, you can save a JPEG in Photoshop as a small, medium, or large file, depending on the amount of information it has and how big you want the file to be.

A JPEG is capable of millions of colors versus the 256 that a GIF offers. In addition, a JPEG boasts continuous tones and gradients of color, and it may be gradually displayed when downloaded. JPEGs are by far the most popular method of saving images on a digital camera (it is one of almost every camera's options).

The biggest drawback to a JPEG, as mentioned previously, is that every time you open and save one, it compresses the file. After numerous opening and closings, these files can become very grainy and not very useful. Keep this fact in mind, and don't open and resave the file more times than absolutely necessary.

#85 How to Size Your Image (Large Versus Small Formats)

This could be considered an easy question to some, but it's also one that is rarely answered correctly. How do you know how large or small to size your image?

When sending digital images for use in magazines, each company has specific sizing requirements. We have sent numerous images to *Videography Magazine* and they require at least 300 *dots per inch* (dpi) for printing and a 5 × 7 or larger image. If we send something larger and with more dpi than that, they can always reduce. Just check with the outlet you prefer and see what they want in size. But what happens if you don't know what they want, and at what size should you store or archive your growing collection of images?

Obviously, the larger the image, the more space it's going to take up, but also the better quality it will have. Photoshop offers a few variables in saving or resizing your image from its original format. The rule of thumb should always be to save as big a file as you can. It is easy to make an image smaller if you originated from a high-quality source, but expanding something that wasn't there from the onset will cause problems.

When in Photoshop, you can save an image as a small, medium, or large file, each with three levels of quality. As an example, a

medium-sized JPEG can be saved as a 4, 5, or 6 setting, with the larger numbers being better quality. The choice should depend on the storage you have and who will be viewing the picture. Generally save the file in the largest setting number in the grouping.

Thumbnails are exceedingly popular on web sites because they take up so little space on the page. If someone wants to see a larger image of the shot, they can click the thumbnail and see an enlarged version. We always save an image as large as possible (8 × 10 usually) and can make enlargements and reductions as necessary.

If a picture is too huge or is stored at 11 × 16 or larger, it becomes cumbersome to send or store. However, portfolios of your best work should be displayed as 8 × 10 printouts or at 1200 dpi on a CD. Our advice, as mentioned earlier in this chapter, is to shoot your images in the Raw format. Although taking up more space, you can print out or store any sized file from this format.

If your photos are to be included in a book with hundreds of others, 4 × 6 is fine, yet prints for a gallery wall should be 11 × 14 or 16 × 20. You can print out any sized image and make it larger, but you run into distortion problems. Use a software program like Photoshop to enlarge or reduce your images for the display medium. Just make sure you have enough to work with.

#86 How to Work with Brightness

Occasionally, something is just not right about your images and you have to start over again from scratch. Usually, if the image is too dark, raising the brightness may correct the situation.

Your brightness control allows you to vary the photo from very light to very dark. Keep in mind that this determines the overall intensity of the image. Any whites in the shot will bloom or glow if the brightness is raised too much. Increasing or decreasing the brightness changes only the lighter objects in the picture. It can more or less make the image appear washed out if too bright.

Figure 8-3 illustrates an image that is too bright (something we've never been accused of). This same thing can be achieved in the video world by adjusting the black "knee" or "setup" in video. Normally residing at 7.5 on the *International Radio Engineers* (IRE) scale, if the blacks are opened up too much, everything in the picture becomes too light or foggy.

This brightness setting really controls very little in an image. Using a software program, take one of your digital images and increase or decrease the brightness. You will notice that it almost is a fine-tuning

Figure 8-3

A photo with its brightness set too high

adjustment rather than a broad one. A digital image can be tweaked using the brightness setting, but it usually isn't global enough to cause a significant change.

A change in brightness is more evident when adjusting the LCD screen on your digital camera. When viewing it outdoors, adjusting the brightness may make the shot more viewable in different lighting conditions. Much like adjusting the rheostat on your car's dashboard, increasing the brightness only makes the lights lighter and washes out the blacks.

#87 How to Work with Contrast

Contrast can best be described as the range between the darkest and lightest shades that exist in an image. On television sets, we've all adjusted the contrast to get a little more detail in the blacks and to generally make the picture more pleasing. This setting is a global one and controls both the lights and darks in an image.

Many years ago, professional photographers shooting black and white film would intentionally overexpose the film and underdevelop it to help reduce contrast. In the digital era, we have a variety of options to control contrast in our finished digital image. Basically, if your picture has mainly gray areas with little black or white, it's considered flat. If your image is mostly black and white, it would be considered too contrast heavy.

Figure 8-4

My, aren't we contrasty today!

#87

In your image editing program, you can make the necessary adjustments to change your brightness and contrast, which will enhance your final image. Normally, in this program you'll have a dialog box where you can fine-tune both your brightness and your contrast levels. You can adjust your contrast level from very contrasty to flat or very flat. The brightness, on the other hand, isn't adjusted as much. Figure 8-4 shows a picture that has too much contrast. Both the lights and darks are compressed more than they should be.

If the contrast or brightness controls cannot improve the digital image to your satisfaction, many image editing programs offer other controls such as curves and levels. It is especially important to remember that when you make these changes to contrast and brightness, you can selectively do so to a given part of the image. It does not have to affect the entire picture.

A good rule to follow when working with contrast: Adjust the picture until the image begins to look very flat, or when your blacks are too deep and dark. Back off from this adjustment slightly and you'll have a pleasing picture. Often in digital photography you may want to adjust your image slightly beyond what you desire and then bring it back to the correct point.

Obviously, the more thought you can give to the overall look of your image before taking the picture will be helpful and less time consuming when tweaking your image on your computer after the image has been captured.

Chapter 9

Other Equipment

#88 How to Use Other Equipment

There's more to digital photography than just a camera. It's the other items that help complete your package. Chapter 9 discusses how to use a tripod, monopod, avoiding using the viewfinder, and the best ways to make your batteries last longer.

#89 How to Use a Tripod

Almost everyone is familiar with the most common type of camera support: the tripod. Available in various sizes, strengths, and prices, the tripod is a useful tool for any level of photographer.

A tripod is an expandable three-legged support that your camera attaches to through a threaded hole in the bottom of your camera. These threads are standard and any camera should fit. A tripod is a necessary piece of equipment when shooting in order to prevent any movement when depressing the shutter or when using the self-timer (if available) on your camera.

The self-timer allows you to compose the picture and push the shutter release button while giving you enough time (usually around 10 seconds) to include yourself in the picture. If you're shooting with a telephoto lens, it's also a good idea to use a tripod or a monopod (a one-legged camera support) due to the size and weight of the lens.

Tripods are manufactured to be compact and light for small- and medium-format cameras. Some tripods are heavy but necessary when shooting with a large-format 4 × 5 film camera. Most professional photographers will choose a sturdy, well-built tripod and use it the majority of the time they shoot.

Fluid head tripods are available that offer smooth pans and tilts because the fluid actually creates a slight drag. These are more suited for video or motion shoots where fluid movement is needed. The amount of fluid in the head may be regulated to control the friction in the move. The more fluid used the smoother the move. The fluid in the tripod head gives it its name — "fluid head." The expense isn't justified for digital photography. When shopping for a tripod, get one that is suited for still photos, not video shots (unless you plan to use the same tripod for both).

Use a tripod when you're shooting a portrait since it enables you to pose your talent, check how the shot looks from the camera, and make subtle adjustments in the subject's head tilt, hair, clothing, or posture.

Check with your local camera dealer or discount store for recommendations on a tripod to purchase based on the camera you're using. In any low light conditions (like other items in life), don't leave home without your tripod (don't tell American Express we said that).

#90 How to Use a Monopod

Camera support is critical and sometimes a tripod isn't feasible or available. Your other option should be a monopod, a second cousin to the tripod with two less legs. A monopod provides a means to help you support your camera with one sturdy leg. We've all seen photographers along the sidelines at a football or basketball game with a monopod attached to their camera that's half the size of a baseball bat.

Monopods can be used for several different reasons, such as when shooting with a telephoto lens, which is typically worth as much and in many cases more than the camera itself. Any telephoto lens is going to be somewhat bulky and heavy, making it difficult to hold up. A monopod attached to a camera, however, can easily be picked up and moved a couple feet when you need to change your shooting location in a hurry without being trampled, such as at a sporting event.

A tripod is also very portable, but in a crowded area it's sometimes difficult to work your way into a group and find enough room to set up the legs of the tripod. You're also more likely to have someone trip over one of the legs or bump into you or the tripod during an exposure.

For a studio photographer, a monopod takes on a different role in the sense that it is not meant to be taken out of the studio. A good monopod will be delivered to a studio unassembled due to its size and will remain in the studio to support medium- and large-format cameras (such as a 4 × 5 view camera).

A camera that's mounted on the monopod slides along a pole to allow you to shoot from various heights. Photographers use a monopod to shoot tabletop work and for shots that cover several feet across the floor of the studio. In many cases, the camera will need to be positioned high on the monopod, necessitating that the photographer stand on a ladder to allow him or her to reach the camera's controls.

The monopod is essential in the studio when shooting with a large-format camera as well as when shooting long exposures. These exposures could be seconds or minutes, depending on the bellows extension and lighting conditions.

#91 How to Avoid the Viewfinder

This may sound like a strange solution, but times will occur when you cannot see the action in the viewfinder yet still need to frame the shot. Although these instances might not be frequent, by resorting to devious means, you can still get the shot.

As an example, if you are with a crowd of people and Brad Pitt walks out of the Mini Mart (you figure out why he's there), you probably will want to get a shot of him (not at him, of him). Because the crowd will have the same idea, everyone will be pushing and shoving to get his photo.

Instead of getting part of his elbow as you are pushed away, hold your camera at arm's length above your head, pointing it down. With the camera set at its widest angle, if you aim in the general direction, you will get the shot. Don't try this with a telephoto lens unless you are sure the subject is framed. We've never missed getting a shot like this because we are above the crowds and our arms add another three or so feet to our height (unless you are related to an orangutan). Obviously, you cannot see in the viewfinder at this height and you will have to trust the camera when you release the shutter.

If possible, snap off as many shots as you can at this height, moving your perspective slightly as the camera shoots away. These will be wide, high-angle shots, but once the images have been saved, use a software program to zoom in and enlarge the subject, cropping out what you don't want. Most of the images in *People Magazine* use this approach because of the stars' bodyguards and crowds of fans that usually follow them. The photographers' job is to get the shot in any way possible.

The same technique works at sporting events when you can't see the action. If you don't want someone to know you are taking their picture, don't hold the camera up to your face and look through the viewfinder. People somehow don't realize you can take a picture without looking through the camera. Instead hold the camera behind your back, at waist level or down by your legs, and take the image.

Figure 9-1

Deceit can still get you the shot.

If you use your camera at its widest setting, the shot will be there. This is a great way to get candids. Just make sure you have releases if you intend to publish the photos later. Figure 9-1 shows how we got a shot by pointing the camera above our heads and aiming it at the subject.

#92 How to Best Utilize Batteries

One thing you can say about batteries, they will fail when you need them most. A battery stores energy to be used later, but somehow that "later" isn't when you want it. How can you make your batteries last as long as possible?

The best thing you can do is avoid buying cheap, no-name batteries. They may save you money, but their life is extremely short. If your camera comes with a special battery, you need to use that one, but buy as many spares as you can afford and keep them charged.

If you have a digital unit that takes store-bought batteries like AA, AAA, or 9 volt, get alkaline or rechargeable cells. Discount stores sell batteries in bulk, so stock up. Never mix dying batteries with new ones because the older fellows will suck the life out of the new ones, much like an angry spouse.

Once you have new and charged batteries, make sure you insert them correctly. When batteries get old and die, take them out of the camera and dispose of them properly; their chemicals are bad for the environment. Keep the camera's battery compartment contacts clean with a pencil eraser, and if you don't intend to use your camera for an extended period of time (longer than a few weeks), remove the batteries. A battery will drain, although slightly, if making contact inside a camera. A bunch sitting in a drawer will last a lot longer.

#93 How to Avoid Memory in Batteries

This brings to mind two important facts about all batteries: memory and storage. Number 1: If you purchase nickel cadmium batteries (chargeable), use them slightly, charge them fully, use them slightly, and charge them fully again. They will develop what is called *memory*, which should be avoided.

Memory is when a battery remembers you only used it slightly so it will only discharge slightly before it dies. You've instilled a bad pattern and it remembers. With memory, you will never see a battery drain completely. Once memory sets it, it's hard to make it forget.

To avoid this, run your batteries all the way down and then recharge them. Even if you have to leave your camera on to do this, let them drain all the way to the point of the camera shutting off before recharging them. In the same manner, let a dead battery charge up all the way before you stop the charging cycle. It can develop memory this way too.

Newer lithium ion batteries do not develop memory. You can use them as little or as much as you like and you will always get a full charge from them. Most cameras now utilize this type of battery.

#94 How to Store Batteries

The second important fact about batteries is storing them at a fully charged capacity. When you are finished using the camera and the batteries are drained, charge them fully and then store them. The amount of drainage over a few months will be slight and you will still have a nearly fully charged battery when you need to use it again.

If you want batteries to last longer before you use them, keep them cold. This means putting them in the refrigerator or even the freezer if you don't need them for a long period of time. However, if you do this, you must warm the batteries to room temperature before you try to use them.

If you are in a hurry and pop them in your camera, they will not last long because they are cold. If someone made you exercise when you were cold, you would move much slower and wouldn't perform as well as if you'd had a proper warmup. The same thing is true about batteries.

If you have a shoot at the South Pole, keep the batteries warm enough so they will last. We usually keep a few spare batteries in our jackets close to our hearts to keep them warm. We're not sure if it's the body temperature or the love we give them that does it.

A battery that lasts one hour at room temperature will only last 15 minutes in below-freezing temperatures. Don't try to make a battery really warm to get twice the use out of it by using a microwave. That will cause other problems.

We aren't saying you try this, but you can check a charge of a battery the way your grandfather did: by touching the battery's contact to your tongue. Yes, you will feel as slight tingle and you'll know there is a little juice left. Just don't try this same trick with your car's battery like we did. When they found our remains two miles away, we were still smoldering.

Chapter 10

Flashes

#95 How Much Can a Flash Do?

Exactly what can you do with a flash and a digital camera? This chapter discusses how to use a flash, how to use a built-in flash, how to use an external flash, and how to use an auto-flash. It discusses using the red-eye reduction mode, a hot shoe flash, a PC or wireless flash, and a fill-in flash. We'll also look at how to diffuse a flash, how to bounce a flash, how to shoot with multiple flashes, how to use reflected light, and how to use bounced light.

#96 How to Use a Flash

One of the greatest inventions in photography has to be the flash. Where else can you travel somewhere and have an instant, portable source of bright light? Whether attached (fixed) to the camera or connected via a hot shoe, the flash will help you indoors as well as out. A hot shoe is a metal slot on the top of your camera that makes a connection with the bottom of your flash. The word "hot" is used because of the electrical contact that is made, and "shoe" because the flash slides in like a foot slides into a shoe.

When you find yourself in a position where you're ready to take your picture and you don't have enough available light, your electronic flash is the answer. The flash on your digital camera, however, does have its limitations. Try to get reasonably close to your subject so your flash will be able to provide enough light. A flash unit on most digital cameras should be able to illuminate and properly expose an image 8 to 12 feet away.

Some cameras have more powerful flashes, but usually not enough to light up your child receiving an award on the opposite side of the auditorium. When we see the flashes going off at concerts or sporting events 200 feet from the subject, we can only hope that the person is shooting digital and not film. They've essentially wasted an exposure on a roll of film compared to a quick review in the camera and immediately detecting your mistake.

The other drawback to a flash is that some move in too close to the subject, overexposing the image and melting them with the searing heat of the flash. If you intend to be closer than four feet, either diffuse the flash or bounce it to avoid creating a permanent shadow on the background.

In many cases, you can purchase an accessory flash for your camera that will provide more flexibility. An accessory flash is simply one that's not built into your camera. Some cameras have a hot shoe adapter that allows the flash to be a little further from the lens, which can help reduce red-eye effects in the subjects' eyes and eliminate annoying shadows behind your subject if they're near a wall. An accessory flash with a sync cord allows you to get the flash high enough to properly light your subject's face and eliminate shadows by having them fall behind the subject. This may not always be practical, but it is an option.

Any time you shoot with a flash, you need to be aware of possible reflections off mirrors, windows, eyeglasses, and any other shiny surfaces. When you point a bright light source at something, reflections will happen (not a nice reflection on you).

On one occasion where an executive of a major corporation needed to be photographed wearing his glasses, we suggested he go to his optometrist and have the lenses removed temporarily for the shoot. This worked well, as no one had a clue that the lenses had been removed. If you try this approach, make sure your subject isn't squinting because their eyesight has diminished. With the magic of a digital camera, you can immediately see if these reflections are a problem. Sometimes just having the talent raise or lower his or her chin slightly will alleviate this concern. Also, moving the subject's glasses up or down slightly can also solve this problem. Check your image and adjust the glasses accordingly.

If you can't eliminate any of the distractions in the background, try changing the angle from which you're shooting. If all else fails, forget trying to use the flash and grab your tripod. The available light may be your only other option, but don't forget to utilize all the available light possible and make any aperture corrections to your camera to allow for more light to reach your subject.

If you're shooting more than one person using your flash, get them as close together as possible. If one person is several feet behind the person in front, the flash may overexpose the person in front, while not getting enough light to the person behind, making them appear dark.

We recently had a situation at a wedding where the bride was wearing white (as she should) and everyone else in the party was dressed in jet black. At dusk, we used the flash, but the light reflected off the white gown, shrouding the rest of the people in darkness. The solution to this was to slow the shutter speed two stops to allow more ambient light to even out the extreme contrast range.

Get in the habit of using your flash outdoors and in. The extra blast of light is rarely wasted. Remember to take a minute and check the camera to see if your lighting is even. When shooting with a flash, try to take an extra shot or two. Extra images can always be deleted later. It may be impossible to get those shots at a later date.

Some people have this apparent third sense and seemingly anticipate when the flash will fire and actually close their eyes. Other people can be photographed numerous times and always manage to have their eyes wide open. Once again, a digital image can be quickly checked for the blinking people.

With most digital cameras, use the auto-flash feature, which will fire the flash automatically when lighting is poor or questionable. The sensor on the camera will determine how much light to output. When shooting portraits, consider using your red-eye reduction feature if this is an option on your digital camera. This feature basically has a preflash lamp that will light just before the main flash. Ideally, the preflash will make the pupils contract just prior to the main flash firing and reduce the red-eye effect caused by the flash reflecting from the retina. You've all seen this where the subject has to hold his or her smile while the preflash fires.

Many digital cameras also have an "anytime flash" or "fill-in flash" mode that is used to illuminate shadows anytime a picture is taken. This works well outside to light a face evenly when the subject's face is partially lit by the sun. Given the opportunity, photograph your subject both ways (with and without a flash), review the results in the camera, and use what works best.

#97 How to Use a Built-in Flash

Since most digital cameras come with a built-in flash, learning how to best use it will make your life a lot easier. Now you'll always have enough light to expose your image.

Some of the most sophisticated models measure the amount of light reflecting back from the object and adjust the amount of illumination to compensate for the light and dark areas in your subject. The *No Flash* mode prevents the flash from firing at all. You might choose this mode if you want to capture an image of your subject or object near a minimal light source such as a candle.

#98 How to Use an External Flash

When we say external flash, we don't mean using a flash outdoors (that would be called "using a flash outdoors"). Instead, we'll consider any flash that is not built into your digital camera by the manufacturer to be an external flash. This could include a small flash unit that is inserted into the hot shoe on the top of your camera, a flash mounted on a bracket (a metal bar) that is screwed into the tripod socket on the bottom of your camera, or a flash on a stand with an umbrella.

One advantage of an external flash is that the light being produced by your flash is not as close to the lens, which will help reduce the chances of getting the dreaded red eye in your pictures. The hot shoe flash is only slightly above and away from the lens, as opposed to a flash on a bracket, which can be several inches to a foot away. This bracket option gives you the flexibility to hold the flash in any position and with a touch of a button will disconnect the flash from the bracket and still have your sync cord (a cable that attaches the flash to your camera, other than a hot shoe) attached.

A flash strobe is a more powerful light source mounted on a sturdy light stand that can extend several feet into the air. You'll typically see this flash used for portraits or groups of people where you want to bounce light onto your subject, making the light much less harsh. The umbrella is pointed in the direction of your subject; however, the flash is not aimed at the subject at all, but rather into the umbrella.

As with any external flash, you'll need to have a sync cord, which plugs into both your flash and your camera. You'll also need to set your ISO, and in many cases when you set the ISO, you'll be given a recommended f-stop based on the distance from your camera to the subject. The most powerful flash units on a stand will have settings for full power, half power, quarter power, and possibly others.

We prefer and recommend the use of a lens shade when shooting with a flash to help eliminate light coming back into the camera lens. Figure 10-1 illustrates a flash strobe and umbrella.

Figure 10-1

A flash strobe and umbrella

#99 How to Use Auto-Flash

As the name implies, auto-flash does everything for you automatically. In this mode, you won't get too much or too little light on your subject.

Cameras with built-in flashes have a variety of settings you can use for various shooting situations. The auto-flash mode allows the camera to set the exposure for you. The camera's meter examines the scene and fires the flash if enough light isn't available. It's smart and knows how much light to use.

Just set the flash in this mode and don't worry about it again—it's automatic.

#100 How to Use the Red-Eye Reduction Mode

If your camera has a red-eye reduction mode, use it when photographing people or animals, especially in dark areas. Red eye is caused by light reflecting from a subject's retina back into the camera. In red-eye reduction mode, the flash fires two to several times in rapid succession. The initial flash causes the subject's irises to shrink, making them

Figure 10-2

My, where has the red eye gone?

smaller and less likely to produce red eye when the actual flash fires a fraction of a second later.

When you press the shutter, it takes a few moments for the picture to be recorded because the flash is firing to reduce any red-eye effects. This takes some getting used to because you may expect to hear the shutter immediately. This pulsating light also distracts the subject because he or she isn't expecting the mesmerizing lights. It's up to you if you would rather your subject have red eye or the blank stare he or she may give you from the light show. Figure 10-2 shows an image of someone shot with red-eye reduction mode.

#101 How to Use a Hot Shoe Flash

If you are familiar with cameras, you know that the hot shoe is the metal adapter on the top or side of your camera. Flash units slide into this and make contact with the metal surface, allowing the flash to fire on command. The hot shoe first became available in the early 1970s and eliminated the need for a PC cord to make the flash do its thing.

These flash units are light, portable, and mounted onto your camera above your lens. Make sure you push your flash into the adapter slot

Figure 10-3

Hot shoes, anyone?

and then slide and secure it in place. The flash may have a sync cord that will run from your flash unit to your camera. The hot shoe should eliminate the need for this because it gets its information from the camera via the hot shoe. Figure 10-3 shows the location of the hot shoe.

Most of these flashes require that you set the ISO on the unit itself. This will provide you with a recommended f-stop you should shoot at, based on the distance from your camera to the subject. You'll need to turn on the power to the flash with a button or switch.

If the power button is not in the on position, the flash simply won't fire. You'll also need to set your shutter speed on your camera to whatever the manufacturer suggests. This recommended shutter speed will normally be in red or have a flash symbol to assist you. If you have any doubts, check your manual.

#102 How to Use the Flash at a Slower Shutter Speed

If the shutter speed is normally 1/125 of a second, the camera will synchronize the light of the flash and your shutter opening. If you need more light because you are in a darkened area, adjust the shutter speed

Figure 10-4

Too fast a shutter speed in too dark an area. The shutter speed should have been set two settings slower.

to a slower setting (less than 1/125 of a second). The shutter will remain open longer and the flash will still fire, giving you more illumination. Figure 10-4 shows an image shot in a factory where the flash fired at its synch speed, 1/250 of a second, but it wasn't enough light to properly fill the void, leaving a dark image.

#103 What Happens If You Use a Faster Shutter Speed?

If, on the other hand, you set your shutter speed too fast for the flash, the shutter fires faster than the flash, showing you only a partial picture, which can be seen in Figure 10-5.

With a digital camera, it's easy to experiment in shooting with a flash at various shutter speeds because you can see the results on your *liquid crystal display* (LCD). Our Nikon's sync speed for a flash is 1/250 of a second. We rarely take an image at that speed; instead we use 1/125 or 1/60 of a second, and the latter gives us two additional stops, something we can always use. This changing of the shutter speed from the recommended setting may not work with a built-in flash, but it works on all hot shoe units.

Since this type of flash is so light and portable, we suggest that it be kept in the camera bag along with extra batteries, sync cords, and any-

thing else you might consider standard. The only way you will thoroughly understand how your flash and camera work is to use them often.

#104 How to Use PC or Wireless Flashes

As digital cameras have made great advances since their inception, so have flashes. The memories on flash units now feature minicomputers that do almost everything except take the picture for you, justifiably raising their prices.

A PC flash is a unit that operates or fires from a cord tethered to the camera. Nothing is really special about it. When it receives a signal from the camera along the wire, it fires the flash. Either one or several can all fire the same time the shutter releases to flood the image with light, but the greatest advances have come in the form of wireless flashes.

The control unit or master usually fits on the hot shoe of the camera. The flash unit or slave can be placed anywhere in the room as long as it is in sight of the master. When the shutter is fired, an infrared beam is sent to the slave and triggers it, all in a microsecond. The great thing about the wireless is in its name; you have no wires to trip over.

On a recent wedding shoot, we used several of these wireless flashes. With all the bridesmaids wearing long gowns, a PC cord could easily be tripped over, sending a flash crashing to the floor. Instead, an assistant would hold a wireless slave flash up high on the left and we would hold another flash above the camera that was connected with a short PC cable. Since our distance was short, no one was going to fall over the cable and our assistant could virtually be anywhere in the church, even behind us, and her flash would fire, all with no wires.

One of the drawbacks to some wireless or noninfrared models is that they are triggered when they see a flash. When the photographer's camera flash fires, the slave unit sees the bright light and goes off also. This poses a problem if other people are taking flash photos too. The slave cannot distinguish between the photographer's camera and anyone else's. A flash is still a flash ("a sigh is still a sigh, the fundamental things apply"). Most tell the audience to refrain from taking flash pictures (rather than singing the refrain like we just did) until the photographer has finished, and then anybody can do so.

We love our infrared flashes because even if you tell people not to take photos, they get caught up in the moment and still do so. Our wireless wouldn't fire, destroying our images because the slave didn't see any infrared signal. If you intend to do weddings, choose the more expensive infrared wireless, while if portraits are your game in a setting where others will seldom take flash photos, an inexpensive light-triggered wireless flash will do. When an assist holds these units, make sure the infrared sensor isn't blocked by his or her fingers.

#105 How to Use a Fill-in Flash

If you only need a little extra illumination to fill in some shadows on someone's face, a fill flash should fit the bill. With only some of its total power being used, it is an excellent supplemental light source. Because it's so versatile, it has many functions.

The *manual flash* or *fill flash* mode triggers the flash even when plenty of light is available. It's best to use this mode when your scene has dark shadows (like the old TV series) you want to lighten. Basically, the fill flash is "filling in the shadows" to even your illumination. Higher-end models allow you to select the amount of light by choosing full power, half power, quarter power, or other possible settings all within a built-in flash.

You can use the *fill flash* mode on your digital camera inside as well as outside. An occasion where you would use fill flash inside would be if you're taking a picture of a subject or object that is in front of a window and have a lot of light *behind* the object and little or no light falling *on* your subject. Figure 10-6 illustrates how dark the subject's face is because the backlight is so strong. Figure 10-7 corrects this problem

Figure 10-6

Anybody need a fill light?

Figure 10-7

All filled with light

by using a fill flash. This also may happen when shooting someone out-doors. The fill flash helps add a little more illumination to the subject's face that normally may have been in a shadow caused by the sun.

Outside you may want to use a fill flash even if the sun is out, but your children are crouched beside their sandbox and the sun is not striking their faces (the only thing that should strike a child). If you're shooting a group of people outside, you don't want them facing directly

into the sun to light their faces because they will squint and you will be shooting a shifty-looking bunch. Instead, you might position the group so the sun is off to the side and use your fill flash to light and in some cases add sparkle to their faces. This is a technique where you can experiment with your lighting and review the results in the camera before making a final determination on how to light your picture. Digital wins again.

#106 How to Diffuse a Flash

Another way of softening the blow from a direct flash is to diffuse it. Diffusion placed directly on the flash will lessen the amount of light from it. This is usually done instead of another method of bouncing light.

People use several different methods to diffuse a flash. Most people choose to diffuse the flash by placing a handkerchief, a piece of tissue, or actual diffusion material over the flash. Some flashes (those made by Vivitar) have a piece of light plastic that slides out over the flash to offer built-in diffusion. These same flashes also allow you to slide the plastic out so the flash bounces off this surface instead of flashing through it.

The same way professional photographers diffuse their lights by putting material in front of them, you can achieve the same result by diffusing your flash, because it is your light source. Both Rosco Laboratories and Lee Filters manufacture diffusion material to use over your flash and lights. With names like Tough Spun (a web-like fabric), Tough Silk (a silky substance), Tough Frost (we think you get the picture), and dozens of others, you can get the look you're after with diffusion.

This same diffusion is also available in non-Tough categories, which means it's not quite as durable as the Tough. Both Rosco and Lee make swatch booklets that have samples of every type of gel and diffusion material they sell. These booklet samples are just the right size to fit over your flash. If you still desire to diffuse your lights, you will have to purchase a sheet of the diffusion material. Most, however, are happy with using the swatch booklet samples over their flashes.

Try taking a picture with each type of diffusion over the flash and note how it changes the quality of light falling on your subject. The closer you get to the talent, the more distinct the diffusion effect will be on the subject.

You can clip or tape the material over the flash, but be sure it doesn't interfere with its output. In past shoots, we've used Bounce dryer sheets (a low-budget shoot) and almost anything else in front of the flash. Although the flash will get warm after repeated firings, it never gets hot enough to ignite the diffusion material (unless you use flash paper). The flash only charges up and fires for a millisecond, and that isn't enough to cause damage. Still, don't look directly at it.

Keep all tape, clips, or whatever you use to diffuse the flash away from the flash itself. Do not attempt to diffuse the flash by placing anything over the flash sensor. When you diffuse the light from your flash by any means, make sure your flash is set in manual mode. Placing anything over an automatic flash will fool it, so be sure to set the flash to manual. Like bouncing, light will be absorbed by the diffusion material, so more power or output is needed for an exposure.

If you don't have anything to diffuse the flash with, you can try to fool it by changing the ISO speed. For example, you could use ISO 400 instead of ISO 200 when setting your flash to reduce the amount of light being output. Figure 10-8 shows Tough Spun placed over the flash to diffuse the light. Figure 10-9 shows a lighter diffusion, Opal Frost, used as diffusion. Although it's difficult to see in a black and white image, a subtle color and texture difference is seen in the actual color photograph.

Take a couple shots and review them in the camera to see if you've successfully diffused the flash and have the image you want. Digital makes it much easier to try numerous diffusion materials over the flash to find the one you like best.

Figure 10-8

Tough Spun over the flash

Figure 10-9

Opal Frost has a lighter punch.

#107 How to Bounce a Flash

Bouncing a flash is a great way to get a soft, even light on your subject without the effects of red eye or harsh shadows. A bounce means letting the flash's light bounce off the ceiling or some other surface to soften the blow.

This is not something you'll be able to do with a point and shoot camera. The flash on these cameras is fixed and you cannot bounce them off anything. When you bounce the light from your flash off a ceiling or other item to diffuse or soften the light, you'll be using an external flash of some sort because its head has the ability to tilt. You can always point your camera upward with a flash and no tilt, but you'll end up shooting the ceiling.

A bounce flash can be mounted on a hot shoe and be set up in different positions, or it can be mounted on a bracket that screws into the tripod socket at the bottom of your camera. This bracket extends to the side of the camera along with a sync cord and gets the flash away from the lens, which can help eliminate red eye. This arrangement also gives you the flexibility to hold the camera with one hand and remove the flash from the bracket with the other. By doing so, you can get the flash high enough in the air that any shadows will fall behind your subject and not be noticeable. Figure 10-9A illustrates the bounce set-up.

Bouncing will diffuse the light that's coming from your flash and give you a much softer light. Depending on the ceiling height or bounce card and the distance that the light from the flash has to travel, you may have to adjust your exposure. When bouncing light from your flash, you may

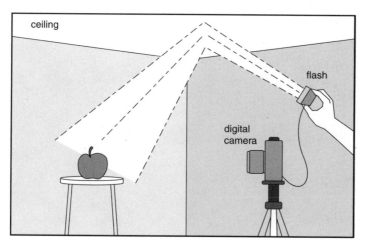

Figure 10-9A

Opal Frost has a lighter
punch.

need to open up your aperture slightly to allow for the distance the light
from your flash has to travel.

When doing the math in these instances, figure out how far the ceiling is away from your flash; let's say five feet. From the ceiling to your subject, the diagonal distance may be 10 additional feet. Even though the actual distance from the subject to the light source is 9 feet, the bounce distance in our example is 15 feet.

Most flashes have charts that tell you which f-stop should be used with a particular ISO speed and distance. The original distance of 9 feet was F5.6 at 200 ISO. The new distance for the bounce requires the lens to be opened an additional stop to F4. The light must travel from the flash head to the ceiling, where some of it is absorbed, and then bounce back down to your subject at a weaker amount of power. That's why you must open another stop.

When you see strobes mounted on light stands and the light is aimed directly into the umbrella rather than being directed towards the subject, the person is doing exactly what we're talking about. The light is being bounced from the umbrella onto the subject and will be much less harsh.

Figure 10-10 shows a subject-to-flash distance of eight feet. The flash is pointed directly at the talent. Note the reflection of the flash or hot spot on the wall directly behind the subject because the light is too harsh to be pleasing. Figure 10-11 shows the same subject, this time with the flash bounced off the ceiling and making the subject-to-flash distance 15 feet. The lighting is now much softer and more attractive. Figure 10-12 shows the lighting when the flash is bounced off a reflective umbrella. The lighting is still very soft, but a little more illumination is evident because of the reflective qualities of the umbrella. Choose the look you like best.

Figure 10-10

Direct flash illumination

Figure 10-11

The flash bounced off the ceiling

#108 How to Use Multiple Flashes

There used to be a saying that the more flash units you had, the more professional you were. Of course, that's not true, but sometimes one flash head isn't enough to get the job done properly.

The time will come when you've met your match as far as trying to light your subject. This enormous object you've been asked to shoot is

Figure 10-12

The flash pointed
into an umbrella
and bounced

not something you're going to be able to capture with your built-in flash. (We're ruling out the possibility, of course, of using available light for this monster.)

The best way to light a subject of significant size is to use more than one flash. Placed at various positions you've predetermined, these extra flashes will give you the coverage you need. Like three-point lighting for portraits, a flash can fire the right amount of light in each position, preventing extra heat from being generated by having lights on all the time. Be careful when placing your extra flash units around your subject to prevent any light from being directed back toward the camera. They can fire directly at the talent, flash into an umbrella, bounce against a white card, or be held by an assistant. In order to have all the flashes fire at the same time during your exposure, you'll need some help.

What you need is a slave or slaves (the lighting kind, not the ones that feed you grapes) that normally have a suction cup to help them stick to your flash as well as a sync cord. The slave, when positioned properly, acts as a sensor, and as light strikes your additional units, your slave will trigger the flash to fire. This all happens much faster than a blink of an eye (which usually happens when someone sees a flash fire).

Before you begin to shoot, check to make certain all your flash units are working properly. Depending on the flash, you may be able to adjust the power output of your different units. This can be helpful if you only need a slight amount of light in a particular area.

Figure 10-13

Multiple lights and umbrellas in action

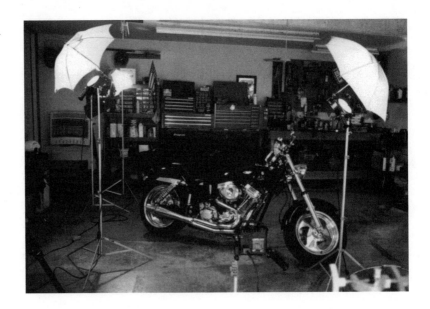

Make sure you have adequate power in the form of batteries to operate your flashes. A weak link in the chain may stop them from firing. Figure 10-13 shows a multiple flash setup.

#109 How to Use Reflected Light

If you want the most powerful form of indirect light, reflecting is the way to go (reflect on it awhile). Getting indirect light from one place to another is done in only two ways: reflecting and bouncing. We'll discuss bouncing in the next solution.

Reflected light is basically illumination that is transferred to another place. You've seen light reflecting off a body of water, you've seen your reflection in the mirror, and you may have seen movie sets where reflectors are getting sunlight where it normally isn't.

Reflected light returns almost 100 percent of the light source's output. Point a flashlight at a piece of shiny metal and you will see the same bright output reflected on the wall. Let's use another example. If you point a light source into a mirror, almost all of that light is reflected where the mirror is pointed; very little of the illumination is absorbed by the mirror. Any high-gloss surface will reflect light rather than bounce it.

On past photo shoots we've used *reflectors*, which are silver (much like aluminum foil) or gold materials for reflecting light. Silver reflectors bathe the subject in a soft, cool light, while a gold reflector provides warmer light, making the subject appear more healthy. Various textured

Figure 10-14

A gold reflector adds warmth to the scene.

silver or gold reflectors have bumps and ridges that send the cool or warm light in numerous directions.

Mirrors are obviously the best reflectors and will send the strongest amount of light back because not all reflectors are created equal. Some are more reflective or powerful than others. A ridged surface scatters the light's rays, making it appear less reflective, which it is, but the light beam is spread over a larger area.

Small make-up mirrors are used on tabletop shoots to send shards of light to highlight and caress the product. The magnification side of a make-up mirror won't enlarge or give you more light, however; it has the same reflective qualities as a regular mirror.

Don't use mirrors as reflectors outside if the sun is your only light source. The sun is extremely hot and will blind, damage, or burn your subject. Even carrying a mirror outside on a sunny day is a dangerous proposition. Instead, if you must use a mirror outdoors, point a light at it and keep the sun away. A silver or gold reflector will do a much better job with the sun and not bake the talent in the process. Figure 10-14 shows a reflector at work.

#110 How to Use Bounce Lighting

Some say a bounced light has a softer output than a reflected light, which is true depending on which surface you're using. Unlike reflected light, a bounce light loses much of its punch in the traveling process.

#110

Figure 10-15

Be happy with your bounce.

When you point a light source at a white card, 40 percent of the light is going to be absorbed by the card, and the other 60 percent will end up at its destination. If you want a softer more diffused light, a bounce is the way to go. Times will occur when you don't want all of the light, just some of it.

If you're shooting a portrait and only have one light source, possibly a flash, put that on the left or right side of your subject to act as a key light. Then place a white sheet of foam core on the other side to act as a fill or bounce. When the flash is on one side and is pointed at the foam core on the other, most of the flash will illuminate the talent's face and the bounce card will give a slight bit of light on the opposite side, creating a pleasing balance of light. If you use equal amounts of light on both sides of the talent (two bounce cards or two flashes), very little modeling will be realized. You want depth and dimension to your talent, not flat, even lighting.

A light can be bounced off any dull surface. Using blue paper will bounce blue light back, orange bounces orange, and so on. If you want softer, broader light, use a bounce to fill in shadows, illuminate large areas with diffused light, or use various types of bounce cards to light your entire shoot. The closer you place a light to a bounce card, the broader your light spread.

If shooting indoors, we always use some form of bounce lighting and very little reflected light. If shooting outdoors, we will reflect the sun's light but create a fill by using bounce lighting.

To more easily remember the terms, with bounce, light is absorbed because the light's rays are *bouncing* around and quite a few get lost in the process. With reflected, almost all the light gets where you want it, such as looking at your *reflection* in the mirror and seeing all of you, not just part of you. Figure 10-15 shows a bounce card used in a lighting setup.

Chapter 11

Image Storage Devices

#111 How to Use Image Storage Devices

Numerous ways exist for storing your newly captured digital images, and you should know what's out there. Chapter 11 will delve into how to store images, how to use floppy disks, and how to use a *Personal Computer Memory Card International Association* (PCMCIA) card. It will cover how to create a photographic CD, how to use a memory stick, how to use smart media cards, and how to use flash cards. The chapter will also explain how to store images on your hard drive, how to store images on a DVD, how to use other storage mediums, and deciding how much memory you really need.

#112 How to Store Images

It doesn't matter which type of camera you have, eventually you'll want to store the images so you can view them later. The time to choose which type of storage media you'll be using is when you're ready to purchase your camera. A lot should be considered and the first thing you should think about is estimating the amount of storage you think you'll need.

Try to evaluate the proportion of high-resolution to low-resolution images you'll take. The more high-resolution pictures you take, obviously the more storage space you'll need. Cameras can generally store 12 to 16 high-resolution pictures in 8MB of storage, twice that many at a medium resolution, and around 100 pictures at a low resolution.

Try to estimate how often you'll be able to move images from your camera and its storage media (temporary storage) to your computer or another type of storage media (more permanent storage). Do you want to store your images to a floppy, a PCMCIA card, a photographic CD, a Memory Stick, a Smart Media Card, your hard drive, or to SuperDisks? A SuperDisk resembles a thick floppy disk with the advantage of storing almost 10 times as much information.

These are choices that may not be simple to make, so do your homework and research. Evaluate how important the size of the storage media is to you. Some types of storage media, such as floppy disks, SuperDisks, and CDs, are inexpensive compared to Compact-Flash or Smart Media.

Normally, you'll want to store images for the long term in some place other than your camera. Keeping your camera's storage as empty as possible allows you to take more images. Once the storage capacity gets full, transfer the images to another, more permanent storage medium.

#113 How to Use Floppy Disks

The name floppy disk was more appropriate when computers required the flexible 5 1/4 magnetic disk. Word processors also required larger 10-inch floppies to make life easier for the user. Today floppy disks are smaller and encased in plastic to prevent damage.

Floppy disks are readable by any computer that has a floppy disk drive and they are also very inexpensive. Floppy disks hold 1.44MB of information and are 3.5 inches wide. The first thing you'll want to do when using one for storage is make sure the disk is not write-protected. If the disk is write-protected, it cannot be written to. When looking at a floppy disk, you'll notice a square hole in the upper-right corner of the disk as you're looking at the label. If the hole is covered by the sliding plastic cover, you can write or add information to the disk. If the cover happens to be moved and you can see the actual hole, the disk is write-protected and cannot be written to.

Floppy disks are fragile and not a permanent means of storing or archiving images. Basically, a floppy is magnetic film in a plastic covering. If you touch this "film" or place it too close to a magnetic source (such as a TV screen, speakers, or a telephone), the stored images may be damaged or corrupted.

Although you have eight options as to how the floppy disk will go into your camera, only one will work. The edge with the medal slide must go in first. If you feel any resistance, do not try to force the disk into the camera. Remove the disk and reinsert it with the medal slide up (that's why the corner of the disk is cut at an angle on the upper-right corner).

When removing the disk you'll need to push a button on the side of the camera. The disk will partially pop out and you can remove the disk.

After you've stored your images onto a floppy disk, be sure to set the write-protect tab so that you won't accidentally write over your saved files. Also, be sure to store your disks in a cool and dry place, away from any device that might send off a magnetic field. Once again, this should not be a permanent means of storage. Floppies are an inexpensive way to save media to be transferred to another, more stable format: the CD.

#114 How to Use PCMCIA Cards

You've all heard the name PCMCIA before, but do you know what it means? It means *Personal Computer Memory Card International Association*. This is why most refer to them as a PCMCIA card.

A few digital cameras use the original Type II PC cards (also known as PCMCIA cards). These cards are larger than the CompactFlash, Smart Media cards, or the Memory Stick media, but they have the capability of being read by any computer with a PC card slot.

The card is inserted into the camera's PC card slot. After images are captured and saved to the card, press the eject button and remove the card. Now you copy your images to your computer's reader or card slot with the software supplied with your camera. PC card slots are commonly found on laptop computers. Just remember, as with any digital/computer tools, these cards are fragile and should be handled with care. They only insert one way, so don't force the issue.

#115 How to Create Photographic CDs

The best storage and archival medium to date is the CD. Images preserved on this laminated piece of plastic cannot be erased, destroyed by a magnetic field, worn out from overuse, or wrecked by touching the surface with your fingers.

A photographic CD has the same appearance as an audio CD, shiny and silver. It is a special type of CD-ROM that can store high-quality photographic images at any given resolution size. You can use the higher-resolution image for large digital prints or for printing purposes in a magazine or advertisement. You also have the option of using a lower resolution for a web page, an e-mail attachment, or as a background or screensaver image on your computer.

Currently, CDs come in two storage sizes: 640 and 700MB. The 640 units have their capacity printed on the label area and are distinguished by a bluish green color (if the burnable type). The larger 700 series is silver and can hold a few extra images and megabytes.

Using a CD writer, you can make copies of your images onto two types of CDs. A CD-R (readable) is a writable one-time media that cannot be erased and is very inexpensive. Once you record images to the disk and finalize it, that's it; it's there for posterity. With a CD-RW (read and writable), you can update and make changes as often as necessary up to 1,000 times. These are slightly more expensive but allow you to constantly update your files.

Although the CDs are extremely durable, they are not indestructible. You should store them in an area that is not subject to extreme temperature changes and humidity, such as a car's interior. Although fingerprints will not affect the images recorded on the disk, other debris can collect on the surface and find its way into the player. If the disk becomes soiled, always clean from the center out with a soft, clean cloth. Don't wipe in a circular motion, rather a straight path from the center outward.

Images are recorded on the inner part of the disk by the center and expand to the outer edge, just the opposite of a record. When your disk has been recorded, you can easily determine how much space has been used by noticing where the lines (pit and fissures) end. Professionally duplicated disks are impossible to judge this way, but any recordable one is quite easy.

#116 How to Use Sony Memory Sticks

All digital images are stored on some form of medium, and Sony has what is called a Memory Stick. Sony Memory Sticks are unique in that they provide at least 32MB of storage for their higher-end digital cameras, while being comparable to the size of a piece of chewing gum, but having less flavor.

Sony has also made these compatible with camcorders, which is a real convenience. When using a Memory Stick, be sure to check that the Erasure Prevention switch is in the off position. Being in the off position will protect any images from being accidentally deleted.

The Memory Sticks can only be inserted one way and have an arrow indicating which direction the Stick should be inserted. When finished capturing your images, remove the Memory Stick by pressing the eject button. You're now ready to copy your images to your card reader provided with the camera using the software supplied.

#117 How to Use SmartMedia Cards

As the name implies, a SmartMedia card is a storage device that has some type of intelligence (like some people we date) because it collects the images and saves them. It also involves media, as in pictures or images.

SmartMedia cards come in one configuration and are clearly identified by their storage capacity, indicated by the number in megabytes written on them. The larger the number, the more information or images it can hold. In addition, this also adds to the expense. When on a shoot that involves storing lots of images, a larger capacity SmartMedia card or numerous smaller capacity cards will be necessary.

The SmartMedia cards are a little smaller than the Compact Flash cards and have similar capacities. When you want to print out the images stored on the card, the files can be loaded onto your computer as with any other digital storage medium, or you can take it to a photography shop and insert it in their computer. We have seen computers that have five little slots in front, one size for each storage medium, making it convenient to have pictures printed no matter which format of storage device you have.

A SmartMedia card can be inserted into your camera in only one way, as one of the corners is actually cut off. This is good because some people manhandle these expensive "chips" and try to insert them in a way they shouldn't. And don't try to use them with dip; they're too crunchy.

When finished shooting, eject the card. Pull the card out of the camera and copy your images onto your computer using your card reader.

Unlike some other storage mediums, you can remove or reinsert the SmartMedia card any number of times, even in the middle of a photo session without harming the data that is stored. Try to do that with a roll of film that is on image number three.

#118 How Flash Memory Works

Electronic memory comes in a variety of forms to serve a variety of purposes. Flash memory is used for easy and fast information storage in such devices as digital cameras. It is used more as a hard drive than *Random Access Memory* (RAM). In fact, Flash memory is considered a solid-state storage device. Solid state means that no moving parts are used; everything is electronic instead of mechanical.

Here are a few examples of Flash memory:

- CompactFlash (most often found in digital cameras)
- SmartMedia (most often found in digital cameras)
- Memory Stick (most often found in digital cameras)
- PCMCIA Type I and Type II memory cards (used as solid-state disks in laptops)

#119 How to Store Images on Your Hard Drive

The easiest and fastest way to store your digital photos is on your computer's hard drive. With today's hard drives holding a minimum of 20GB, that's an awful lot of images. But is this really the best place to store everything?

Hard drives will probably hold as many images as you can collect. It's a storage medium that is readily available and easily upgradeable in interior and exterior drives, and you can call up an image at will. However, it's still not the best solution for long-term, archival storage. The main reason for this is because hard drives are magnetic and can still fail.

In the past when using your computer, how many times has your hard drive crashed? Ours has crashed quite frequently because we add and delete files constantly, but luckily only one time has our hard drive been corrupted and left the images inside in danger of being lost forever. Fortunately, intelligent computer people out there can help retrieve these images, but it is a long process of removing a number of photos from one hard drive and transferring them to another.

We believe that a hard drive is a great interim storage medium, in that it's not the final resting place of all your prized photos. Instead it's just the second step. The first step is obviously saving them on your camera's storage device. As soon as possible, free up your camera's memory and save the photos to a computer's hard drive. This will allow you to look at them later and sort through what you want and don't want. We rarely delete any images from the camera until everything has at least been saved to the hard drive. With the camera's memory now free (once everything is in the hard drive), we can resume shooting images. Normally, we take our laptop computer on location to a shoot and save everything to its 30GB internal drive.

Once all the images are in the hard drive, we delete the ones we know we will never use. Some that may be in question (we call them our "possibles") are kept on the drive and the selected ones are stored on a more permanent medium: a CD-ROM. We try not to finalize the CD until we have enough images on it (we can then add more at a later date), but most 700MB CDs are cheap enough and store at least 20 images. CD drives may crash, but a CD will always function unless it is damaged (which is why we always burn two copies of each and store them in different places).

When storing, adding, and removing images on a hard drive constantly, make it a habit to defragment your hard drive frequently. A hard drive will store bits (or bytes) and pieces of files all over the place (it doesn't matter to you where it keeps them as long as it *keeps* them). A drive defragmentation will clean up a drive and allow you to add more files and achieve a quicker retrieval time. This doesn't hurt a drive; in fact, it's actually good to do it often. We defragment ours after every new project. To defragment a PC, right click on "my computer" and select "manage." A menu with defragment will come up and simply select the drive you wish to defragment. This process may take a few minutes to several hours depending on how much information is on the hard drive.

There you have it. A hard drive is a great place to store images in the process of sorting, but use something more permanent as your archival method, as we mention in the next solution.

#120 How to Store Images on a DVD

A *digital versatile disc* (or DVD) is one of the newest ways to save a large amount of images. A one-sided blank *DVD-recordable* (DVD-R) can hold 4.7GB of information compared to a maximum of 700MB for a CD-ROM.

The same one-sided DVD is also called a DVD-5 in the industry because it holds approximately 5GB (that's 5,000,000 bytes). A DVD-9 is a two-sided DVD that holds approximately 9GB. With this phenomenal amount of storage, you can archive a pile of images.

Like CD-ROMs, DVDs also come in rewriteable forms called DVD-RW (for read/write). Also, like CDs, DVDs can be added to as long as they aren't finalized, which ends the writing process.

The only drawback at present is that not everyone owns a DVD burner. Of course, not everyone has a DVD player in their home or on their computer. The DVDs that you burn (not the ones that are mass produced like the kind you rent) will not play in everyone's DVD drive. Since the technology is still new (as of this writing), we are told that a burned DVD will play in 85 percent of the DVD players made in the last two years. That's not too bad, but it isn't the same as 99.9 percent of all CD-ROM players which is true about CDs.

DVDs offer a menu system that will take you to any file on the DVD when inserted into a player. The CD menu system only works when played back in a computer (which is probably the only place you'll ever open them). You can't insert a CD in a DVD player and expect to play it. A computer is the only place you can view images. If a client wants to see the photos you took using his or her home TV set, a DVD is a better method, although newer DVD players will also play CD-ROMs.

DVD technology is still evolving and soon it will replace the CD-ROM. If you need a large amount of storage, DVD is the way to go, once everyone has access to a burner.

#121 How Much Memory Do I Need?

This is another one of those questions that only you can answer, but we'll try to give you a hint in this solution.

If you do a large amount of shooting and save most of your work, you're going to need more storage than most. On the other hand, if you use very little, a less expensive, smaller capacity device will work fine. In this solution, we'll talk about what's currently available in camera memory capacity. As in computer memory, the prices fluctuate frequently and it's best to purchase larger amounts when the prices are down.

Memory cards come in sizes as small as 8MB (which doesn't hold a heck of a lot) and increasing to 16, 32, 64, 128, 256, 512, and 1GB. You may notice that these storage capacity numbers are the same as computer memory. Prices will drastically increase as the amount of memory enlarges.

We use 256 and 512MB cards because they hold a lot of images. A 512MB card costs twice that of a 256MB card (and it does hold twice the information). As mentioned earlier, prices do fluctuate, so shop around for the best deal.

The more memory you own, the less often you'll have to empty it and add more, but the average photographer will never fill a 1GB card unless you're taking thousands of images at a sitting. We would still prefer having two 512MB cards over a 1GB card (2 times 512 is 1,024 — actually more than a gig at the same price) because if anything happens to the card (if it's lost or corrupted) we would still have a backup. These memory cards can get damaged if abused, dropped, or manhandled. It's an expensive piece of electronics, so treat it with care. Like film, if anything happens to your memory card, you've lost your photos. Our advice is to buy smaller memory modules and get more of them.

Chapter 12

Digital Editing

#122 How to Digitally Correct Your Images

Sometimes we are happy with the way our images look when we view them for the first time on the *liquid crystal display* (LCD) screen. Through editing, however, we can make the photos better (faster, stronger, and more lifelike). We will examine the ways this is possible in this chapter, including how to color correct an image, how to transform an image, how to resize an image, and how to save an image in a different format. We'll also discuss how to increase brightness, how to control contrast, how to use a *Universal Serial Bus* (USB) connection, how to use a FireWire connection, and how to use an image database. You'll also learn how to transfer images directly from your camera or card reader, how to find out if you need a scanner, how to crop an image, how to remove dust and scratches, and how to enhance an image.

#123 How to Color Correct an Image

It's rare that an image, once shot, is perfectly color balanced. Sometimes it's the flesh tones or even the entire look of the picture that's off. This is where color balancing comes into play.

It's not uncommon to look at your digital image on your computer and feel that the color isn't exactly the way you'd like to see it. For instance, pictures taken in the snow may appear to look blue. This is normal with any camera whether it's a top of the line digital camera or an inexpensive point and shoot camera using film.

The image may appear too blue because the daylight color temperature is far too high (or blue) on the Kelvin scale (somewhere around 10,000 degrees K). This is never a problem when shooting snow indoors because the white isn't pulling more blue from the sky. You will, however, have other problems if shooting snow indoors. With your digital image, you can easily adjust color using your image editor's Color Correction tool.

Your image editor may have controls that allow you to change the color in your highlights, shadows, and middle tones separately. This is ideal because you may not want to change the overall color of your picture, just specific parts.

The key here is to make any color adjustments in small increments. If you remove or add too much, it's possible to put it back in, but it's less time consuming if only tiny bits of color are added or subtracted. Color correction needs to be broken down even further into two elements: hue and saturation (or chroma).

Hue is basically the color of the subject. Is it blue, red, or green? The saturation or chroma is the intensity of color in the shot. Is the blue light, medium, or dark blue? These terms are important when color correcting so you know which elements of the color you need to adjust.

Hue is usually a larger and grander type of color correction. A shot of someone looking orange needs a global change. If a person's skin looks pink or too green, adjusting the hue and dialing in the correct flesh color is the only way to compensate. Adding more intensity to the color will only make matters worse.

On the other hand, if the flesh tones look a little pale and lifeless but still flesh-like, adjusting the saturation or chroma will bring in *more* or *less* of the particular color instead of *changing* it, as the hue does. Once you know the differences between hue and saturation, the changing is easy and up to your perception.

Experiment with the color until you have the results you're looking for and be sure to click OK to apply and save your changes.

#124 How to Transform an Image

When we say transform, we mean to change an image into something else. It could be a poorly shot or exposed image that could be improved through digital manipulation.

Photo restorers take a photograph whose colors are faded and transform it into what the image may once have been. Hundreds of color photos we took in the 1970s and 1980s have flesh tones that are now red. By using filters in software packages, the red cast may be removed and a more normal pallor returned to the subject.

As an example, we found a picture in a drawer (it just goes to show you should stay out of your drawers). The picture had a red cast because the dyes had faded and the majority of the red dye still remains. The image looked wonderful when it was taken in 1979.

By using MGI PhotoSuite III SE, we scanned this 35mm photograph and, using a two-step process, we corrected the flesh tones. Under *Touch-up Filters*, we chose the *Color Adjustment* setting. We then set the *Cyan-Red* level to -4, the *Magenta-Green* level to -54, and the *Yellow-Blue* level to -97. The order you do this in doesn't really matter. It's a back and forth tweaking process.

For the second step, we went back to *Fix Colors* under the *Touch-up Filters* setting and set the *Hue level* to -17, the *Saturation* to +21, and the *Value* to -19. Now you would never know the difference.

#125 How to Resize Your Image

If your original digital photo is too large or too small, it may be resized using a number of software programs. In our example we'll use Adobe Photoshop, but others will do just as well.

In Photoshop, open the photograph in question. Under *Image*, select *Image Size*. You now have a number of choices. You can view the width and height in pixels or percent. You may compress or elongate the width and height by changing the values in this top part of the box.

Because we want to keep the same aspect ratio (width to height), we are more interested in the lower section of the box, *Document Size*. You can now adjust the height, width, and resolution of the image by typing in the size or sizes you desire. We usually choose inches from the drop-down box on the right, but if you prefer you can choose from percent, cm (centimeters), points, picas, or columns depending on your specific need.

If you check *Constrain Proportions*, which we usually do, the picture will remain in the same height-to-width proportions so nothing gets distorted. Once you select OK, any size you type in will adjust accordingly. If you aren't satisfied with the results, choose *Step Backwards* in the *Edit* menu and start again.

#126 How to Save an Image in a Different Format

Since clients are people too, they will change their mind often. We've sent images in every format under the sun, because the client decided they didn't want a Targa file and instead wanted a TIFF.

It really doesn't matter what format you chose to save a file in, just make sure it is of high enough quality or resolution. The format is relative, so keep everything in a higher or more *dots per inch* (dpi) mode when you shoot.

Using Adobe Photoshop again (others will also work), we're going to change our massive 12.6MB JPEG file to a TIFF file. Under the File menu, select *Save As*. Look for the word *Format* and select *TIFF* from the pull-down menu. Any other choice can be made here also.

The new image, now a TIFF, is 94.4MB; the file is almost 8 times its size. But if this is what the client wants, that's what it will be.

#**127** How to Increase Brightness

Although all of you are extremely bright, we'll add a little bit of education to our photos and increase their brightness. In other words, we'll change an underexposed image to that of a properly exposed one by raising the brightness level. Unless you intentionally want to overexpose a picture, increasing the brightness on a dark image is a better solution.

Adjusting the brightness is the same in Adobe Photoshop and MGI PhotoSuite III SE. Open the offending image and in Photoshop, under *Image,* select *Adjust* and look for *Brightness/Contrast* as one of the options.

With the box open and *Preview* checked, slide the bar until you are satisfied with the brightness, which can be anywhere from -99 to +99. Usually, only a slight adjustment is necessary in brightness levels before you will notice any underexposed picture start to wash out.

We find that an increase of +10 to +15 is sufficient to lighten an extremely dark picture. To better achieve the perfect balance, you also need to adjust the contrast; these two work hand in hand. The next solution discusses contrast. Figure 12-1 shows an image that is underexposed. In Figure 12-2, the brightness has been increased.

#**128** How to Control Contrast

Contrast is a more global adjustment to a digital image. Whereas brightness tends to wash out a picture quickly, an adjustment in contrast is more pleasing on the eye, making the blacks lighter or deeper in your image.

As mentioned in the last solution, brightness and contrast adjustments work together in that you will be adjusting both, rarely just one or

Figure 12-1

Living in the dark, an underexposed image

Figure 12-2

With the brightness increased, the image is now properly exposed.

#128

the other. It doesn't matter which you adjust first, but the largest gain or decrease will be in the contrast level.

Using the software program of your choice, load the image and select Brightness and Contrast. The scale also ranges from −99 to +99 with most results being in the −30 to +30 range depending on the picture. Figure 12-3 looks mushy because no contrast exists between the lights and darks. By raising the contrast +32, the image as shown in Figure 12-4 looks much better (the image—not the subject).

Figure 12-3

Compressed contrast muddies up the image.

Figure 12-4

With an increase in the contrast, the picture is more appealing.

#129 How to Use USB Connections

Almost every computer has a USB port or connection to accept input or the transfer of signals. This port is where printers, dongles, scanners, external drives, and disk readers are connected to your computer.

Being much faster than a parallel or serial connection, the USB port is a speedier way of getting images onto your computer. But as with all computer-related equipment, it doesn't take long for it to become outdated.

We have loaded tens of thousands of images from our cameras, scanners, and card readers onto our computer via the USB port. The transfer speed was relatively fast and at the time it was the quickest way to complete the process. Having several devices needing a USB connection was never an issue because they could be daisy chained (one device can be plugged into another and the signal loops through).

In an effort to speed up the transfer time of larger photo images, the FireWire port was introduced, which doubled the speed, making the USB port slow and lethargic. The FireWire connection will be discussed in more detail in the next solution.

Not wanting to be outdone, the USB people have devised the USB 2 connection. It looks like a regular USB port, but it exceeds the speed of FireWire (only slightly) and is light years faster than the old USB port. Newer computers feature this USB 2 connection, which is backward compatible, meaning it will accept either USB or USB 2 devices.

When purchasing any external device to attach to your computer, look at the connection it offers: USB, USB 2, or FireWire. Get the fastest connection your computer can handle and you'll save a great deal of time in the transfer process. The time you save will add up, allowing you to spend your free time doing something more exciting, such as taking more digital images.

#130 How to Use FireWire Connections

The FireWire or IEEE-1394 cable, which is also known as iLink (Sony's name for it), is a speedy way to get signals out quickly and into your computer. FireWire got its name from the fact that it transfers visual information (like photos and real-time, full-screen video) as well as two separate audio channels (stereo) and a reference signal (time code). We're only concerned with digital photos, but the connection does handle so much more.

After using the USB port for so long, FireWire was a dream come true. A massive 36MB photo would take only a few moments to transfer, much like a cable modem excels over a 28.8 phone modem.

FireWire cables come with three possible end connections, so you need to make sure you have the correct size on each end of the cable. A 4-, 6-, or 12-pin connection is what's available at present.

Our 80GB external hard drive accepts a six-pin input, but our Dell laptop computer needs a four-pin output. We purchased a cable with a six-pin on one end (looking much like a USB connection) and a four-pin on the other.

Also, one of our cameras has a six-pin output and the other has a four-pin. We have cables in all different lengths and end connections, so we can daisy chain the camera into the hard drive and the drive into the computer. These cables currently are in the $30 to $50 price range and obviously are necessary in the transfer process.

Get the fastest connection you can afford and soon there may be FireWire 2 (or would it be Son of FireWire?)

#131 How to Use Image Databases

Occasionally, you may need an image of something quickly and you are unable for whatever reason to shoot it. That's where an image database or stock library comes into play.

Numerous companies that advertise in trade magazines, in brochures, or on the Internet offer the sale or lease of digital images for a fee. The fee charged depends on the end use of the photos and the length of time you'll be using them. The price could be inexpensive or extremely pricey depending on the company and your purpose.

As an example, we needed images of flying saucers for a Y2K seminar back when people thought that the world was going to end when all computers crashed. We didn't have any images of flying saucers lying around, so we needed to purchase them. Never wanting to tell a client "We don't have it," we promised, "We'll find it."

After spending hours on the Internet and days on the phone, we located a company that had what we were looking for. Their fee of several hundred dollars for one color image that we would project on the screen at the conference included them finding the image, burning the photo to a CD, shipping it overnight to us, and our right to display it publicly.

When the conference was over, we had to return the CD; we just rented it. For that brief 25 seconds, we spent a lot of money, but that's what the client wanted (not us spending her money, getting the flying saucer photo). When contacting stock photo or image database companies, find out the fees involved. It may be more expensive than you realize. Make sure you tell them what your intended use is (don't lie), how long you'll need it (as short as possible), and what your budget may be.

If you only have $30 to spend for this image, tell them up front so you don't waste everybody's time. Perhaps in order for them to get the business, you both could reach a comprise and spend only $50.

Pricing aside, check out the image databases on the Internet. If you need photos of volcano interiors, archival images, or shots of the surface of the moon, an image database will save you the time, expense, and possible danger of shooting it yourself. Just give yourself enough time in the project. It may take a while.

#132 Should You Transfer Images Directly from Your Camera or Use a Card Reader?

You should always view your camera as a temporary storage area, not a permanent one. Naturally, once you've captured an image, it is saved in the camera, but keep the image only until you can transfer it to any type of storage medium you choose. By storing images in your camera, you're taking up valuable space that could be used for capturing additional photos. You not only limit the number of pictures you can save when you don't remove them from your camera, but you also restrict the number of high-resolution images you'll be able to capture.

Your digital camera should be used to capture and store your images only until you have saved them elsewhere. You never know when a photo opportunity might present itself and you grab your camera to shoot only to realize you're out of storage space.

It's a simple and quick process to review the images in your camera, delete those that you don't want or need, and transfer the images you want to keep. But when you transfer those images, should you hook the camera directly to your computer, or should you use a card reader?

Higher-end cameras have USB or FireWire (IEEE 1394) cables that connect directly to your computer. Your computer can then capture these images, but a USB port is slow, especially if trying to transfer high-resolution files.

Card readers have become inexpensive. Your camera's storage card is placed in this reader and your computer sees it as another hard drive.

Depending on the connection, you may be able to transfer images faster with a reader card and a USB 2 connection (which is now faster than FireWire).

It causes no harm to your camera if you connect it directly to your computer, but sometimes on location, we find it easier to pull the storage card, pop in a new one, and transfer the data on the first card via a reader card to a hard drive or CD. This allows us to continue using the camera rather than tying it up in the transfer process. Reader cards can be purchased for around $20 and are easily worth the cost.

#**133** Do I Still Need a Scanner?

Now that you have a digital camera, why would you need a scanner? This is a good question, and only you can answer it. When was the last time you used a scanner or wished that you had one?

If you can't recall, we would conclude that you probably don't need a scanner unless you feel there may be a need for one in the near future. As you're probably aware, many manufacturers make it tempting to own a scanner because they're "part of the package." You've probably seen the ads or you may even own a combination printer, copier, fax, and scanner. No doubt exists as to whether these units are the most convenient (it beats having four different pieces of equipment cluttering your computer area) and the price makes them affordable.

Hewlett-Packard offers an all-in-one printer, copier, and scanner for $147. This is a great price considering what you can do with just one piece of equipment, but these machines do have a downside. If your scanner quits on you and you need to have it repaired, you're also without a printer, copier, and fax machine. This may or may not be a drawback for you, especially if you have someplace you can go to have the unit repaired quickly, as opposed to sending it back to the manufacturer.

If you can transfer images directly from your camera, you won't need a scanner. But if you want to send your digital photographs to some other source using a scanner and a software program, you can incorporate both.

In the acquisition mode, we no longer use our scanners for digital photos. But if we are hired to incorporate existing artwork into our layout, the scanner is invaluable. Just make sure you have enough dpi capability on your scanner to handle large photographs, usually 2,400 dpi and up.

#134 How to Crop an Image

The term "crop" is known by most people as being something other than what grows on a farm. Cropping means to close in on a particular portion of an image, in turn making that area larger. Therefore, cropping means getting a larger look at a smaller area of the image.

The ability to crop an image is instrumental in drawing attention to your main subject. By eliminating any part of the original image that is distracting, you create a more interesting picture. Depending on your image editor, you may have more than one option when you decide to crop your photo. You may have a special cropping tool or a more traditional tool that is rectangular and crops out everything outside of the area you've selected.

The rectangular cropping tool often resembles a series of dotted lines that will indicate the area you want to keep. By clicking the tool on a particular point and dragging it, you can create a square or rectangle of any size. When you alter an image by cropping, it's important to save the original because once you've cropped your image, it has changed from its original format.

You can enhance and be creative with your cropping tool by eliminating unwanted cars, people, signs, too much sky, and many other additional unwanted and unnecessary objects. Some people just prefer to blow up or enlarge a certain area on a picture. By keeping the photo the same size, you are essentially enlarging the image that fills that space when cropping.

The digital advantage is that you shoot your subject when the opportunity presents itself and then make any changes to it later on your computer. Some digital cameras even allow you to crop an image on its viewing screen, saving time spent on the computer later. It doesn't matter when the cropping occurs, in the camera or on the computer.

It's also important to remember that when cropping for whatever reason, the image should still be composed and balanced correctly. We can sometimes get a little "crop happy" by cutting out too much of the background in order to zoom in on the subject. A small amount of background is necessary in any picture to help set the subject off or to establish the environment.

When shooting images for legal purposes, such as scars on victims from an accident, we always shoot as wide as possible to ensure the environment or surroundings are established. The images are later cropped, but not so tightly just to show the scar or mangled bumper.

People still need a reference. Being too close, the viewer might not be able to distinguish the item in the digital photograph.

Cropping is a powerful tool and some people crop too much. Instead, show a little bit more than you think is necessary. You can always crop again later.

#135 How to Remove Dust and Scratches

Dust and scratches are devastating to film and digital images. The lush colors on the printed image are marred by white flecks and jagged creases that run through the pristine smile of our favorite Aunt Martha. Luckily, problems like this are no longer an issue in digital imaging.

Older photographs may be restored using this method, or your new digital images can be cleaned up. Obviously, scratches won't occur in a digital photo, and anyone can digitally correct problems in older, printed images.

Most image editors have a Dust and Scratches command that eliminates scratches, dust spots, and other minor defects. For example, in Photoshop, you would choose *Filter > Noise > Dust and Scratches* and then use the sliders in the dialog box to adjust the preview image to obscure the dust and scratches.

In the program MGI PhotoSuite III SE, the solution to removing dust and scratches is easy. Once the image has been scanned, select the *Scratches* menu bar. Clicking this displays a slider bar.

The closer you go to the left, or to 0, the smaller the correction brush. As you move toward the right, the brush size gets larger for those nasty creases. Then by simply clicking on the scratch, the pixels seem to blur and the scratch is removed. This takes some trial and error until you achieve the result you are looking for.

The scratch or dust problem isn't really removed; instead it is disguised or covered up. By blending the background colors or hues, you effectively eliminate the problem. The before Figure 12-5 illustrates the offending scratch and the after Figure 12-6 shows the scar permanently removed.

You may want to adjust the preview zoom ratio until you can clearly see the area containing the defects. By enlarging, you can more easily blend the correction tool.

It's possible you can also minimize these conditions by slightly blurring the image if your image editor does not contain the needed fea-

Figure 12-5

A scratched
image

Figure 12-6

An unscratched
repair

tures. Depending on how and where the images are used and at what size, many of the defects may not be visible.

#136 How to Enhance an Image

Enhancing an image basically means making it better than it was before. The first thing you need to do is determine what you'd like to do with the image to improve upon what you may have. Irregardless of what version you're using, thanks to Photoshop you can enhance your images in numerous ways.

One way of enhancing a photo is by increasing or decreasing the contrast as well as the brightness. Removing blemishes, scratches, or anything in your image area can be easily accomplished in the same way. You can remove the red-eye effect you often get when using a camera with a built-in flash.

You may want to sharpen or blur an image, or crop a photo to eliminate something or someone in your picture. Why not think about changing your background or creating a completely new one? An image may be more appealing if it is rotated, or you may want to add text to your image to personalize it.

Use your color correction tools to get the exact color rendition you want in your final image. The special effects tools can not only enhance your image, but create an image that's totally unique.

Beware of the distortion tools! We mention this only because we're talking about enhancing an image and with the distortion tools, the effect is normally not an enhancement. Actually, it is quite the opposite!

#136

Chapter 13

Software Programs

#137 How to Choose a Software Program

With so many different software programs available for manipulating digital images, how do you know which one is right for you? This chapter will explain what a few software programs do to help you best make a decision. This chapter will demonstrate how to use digital film formats, how to use iPhoto™, how to use Paint Shop Pro, and how to use MGI PhotoSuite III. The chapter will also cover how to use Adobe Photoshop, what it can do for you, and what you can do with a low-end program.

#138 How to Use Digital Film Formats

Although they are not really software programs, we've never really discussed the digital film formats available. Most of us will be using a digital camera that records the image in megapixels, whether it is a standalone camera or a digital back for a medium-format camera.

We've mentioned the storage methods once the image has been captured in the camera, but once you get into a software program, you can save your file in any number of different formats. These include *Joint Photographic Experts Group* (JPEG, jpg), Targa (tga), *tagged image file format* (TIFF, tif), *Portable Network Graphic* (png), the Compuserve *graphics interchange format* (gif), Windows Bitmap (bmp), i format (fpx), PC Paintbrush (pcx), Sting (stng), Sun Raster (ras), *Seattle Film Works* (SFW), and Photoshop's *Portable Document Format* (pdf).

Each one of these formats saves the file slightly differently, and explaining the differences between each one is beyond the scope of this book. Try saving an image in each of these different formats and see how it differs in file size and clarity.

#139 How to Use iPhoto

A number of software programs are available and iPhoto is easy to use. iPhoto is dedicated to the Mac user environment and is a very unique and dependable tool.

Digital cameras are revolutionizing the way we take pictures. Now Apple is providing the missing link to modernize the way we save, organize, share, and enjoy digital images. Software programs allow you to get more out of your digital pictures.

iPhoto lets you import, organize, edit, and improve your digital pictures, as well as share them in a number of different ways. Once you see what iPhoto can do with digital pictures, you may never go back to using a film camera again.

Just plug your camera into your Mac's USB port and iPhoto automatically imports, catalogs, stores, and displays your photos on your screen. Simply drag your mouse, and iPhoto magically grows or shrinks your photo thumbnails right before your eyes. Now you can view individual shots in greater detail for precise cropping. If you desire to see hundreds of photos on the screen at once, or want to quickly scroll through thousands to find the one you're looking for, iPhoto may be the answer. Gone are the days of scavenger hunts to find pictures on your hard drive.

iPhoto lets you easily organize your photographs into digital birthday, vacation, or wedding albums for easy retrieval. Sharing and enjoying them is a cinch, too. Push one button to display them in a beautiful full-screen slide show, accompanied by your favorite music. You can also easily e-mail them to friends or print them on your ink-jet printer. If you use a Mac, you should further research this product to discover the benefits it may offer you.

#140 How to Use Paint Shop Pro®

Paint Shop Pro offers probably the easiest, most affordable way to achieve professional results without spending a fortune (normally less than $100). With this photo editor, you can achieve high-end professional images that don't take a lifetime to learn. Also, avoid being taken in by other editor programs such as slow, cookie-cutter packages that tie you to templates and eliminate your creativity. You can purchase Jasc Software's Paint Shop Pro from your local retail stores or from the Internet.

Before considering purchasing Paint Shop Pro, decide if you need the home or business version. With Paint Shop Pro you can

- Retouch, repair, and edit photos with easy-to-use, high-quality, automatic photo-enhancement features
- Create and optimize web graphics with built-in web tools, artistic drawing, and text tools
- Design basic animations with Animation Shop 3
- Easily add custom images to your home and business graphics projects
- Save time with productivity tools such as grids, guides, alignment, and grouping
- Expand your creativity with over 75 special effects
- Share photos electronically with friends and family via e-mail, web sites, and photo-sharing sites

Some of the general tools included are used for painting, drawing, adding text, image editing, layering, screen captures, watermarks, and additional file formats. The artistic effects include special effects, filters, and the picture frame function.

Lastly, the productivity tools are the visual browser, multiple-level undo/redo, multiple image printing, the batch file format, the conversion overview window, and save workspaces. As with any new program, try it and see if it suits your needs, but with a package like this, it's hard to beat.

#141 How to Use MGI PhotoSuite III

The MGI PhotoSuite III software program is inexpensive and often comes bundled with scanners. Our version, MGI PhotoSuite III SE, is menu driven (like most programs) and allows quite a bit of image manipulation.

Images can be input through a scanner, digital camera, library, Kodak PhotoNet online, or through a computer. Once the image is displayed, click the *Prepare* tab and you can begin changing it.

Rotate and Crop, *Touch-up*, *Special Effects*, and *Stitching* are the four main selections from which to choose. *Rotate and Crop* gives you the choice of *Rotation*, *Flip*, *Straighten*, and *Crop*, each with fine-tuning perimeters.

The *Touch-up* choice offers *Enhance*, *Remove Red-eye*, *Remove Scratches*, *Remove Blemishes*, *Remove Wrinkles*, and *Touch-up Filters*. Each of these, with the exception of *Touch-up Filters*, displays a slider bar and a brush size in which to make the necessary changes. *Touch-up Filters* takes you to another menu where you can choose a specific filter from a pull-down menu. *Brightness and Contrast*, *Scratch Removal*, *Fix Colors*, *Sharpen*, *Soften*, *Invert*, and *Color Adjustment* allow you to change specific attributes in the digital image.

By hitting the *Back* button, you can return to *Special Effects,* which opens a category, *Natural,* and a pull-down menu that offers *Fog, Glass*, *Snow*, *Wind*, and *Smoked Glass* as your filter choices. If, instead of *Natural,* you select *Artistic*, more options such as *Mirage*, *Emboss*, *Posterize*, *Cartoonize*, *Painting*, *Crystallize*, *Splatter*, *Swirl*, *Ripple*, and *Spherize* will do the particular effect when selected.

Geometric only has three selections: *Mosaic*, *Randomize*, and *Tile,* while *Enhancement* only has two: *Gaussian Blur* and *Smart Blur*. *Lens* changes the look of the photo by offering *Warm*, *Cool*, *Sepia*, *Tan*, *Moonlight*, and *Antique*. Each of these makes global changes with no fine-tuning.

Finally, *Painterly Effects* brings more extreme manipulation with *Frosted Glass*, *Canvas*, *Rain*, *Grass Effect*, *Weave*, and *Brick*. Each of these has a fine-adjustment setting.

Stitching allows you to piece together several images and make one new image. The Platinum Edition is the upgrade from SE and offers many more choices. We've been fortunate with the power of SE and haven't even had the need for most of what it has to offer.

As with any software program, play around with it to see what it can do, so when the need arrives you'll better know your capabilities.

#142 How to Use Adobe Photoshop

By far the most popular image-editing software, Adobe Photoshop is so comprehensive that finding a designer or a computer artist who is not working with it on a regular basis would be extremely difficult.

The initial impression from most people using Adobe Photoshop is that it is user-friendly and can do almost anything you might require. On the surface you'll find that this is the tool that will simplify all your photo-editing needs. The more you use and experiment with Photoshop, the more obvious it will become that it contains a vast amount of information to learn and tools that you never imagined existed.

Adobe Photoshop software, the professional image-editing standard, helps you work more efficiently, explore new creative options, and produce the highest quality images for print, the Web, and anywhere else. Create exceptional imagery with easier access to file data; streamlined Web design; faster, professional-quality photo retouching; and more.

Photoshop requires a lot of *random access memory* (RAM), at least 96MB. If you can't launch Photoshop because of a memory error, you have three options:

- Try restarting your computer. This will reset everything and you can start from scratch.
- Free up more RAM by closing anything else that may be operating.
- Since RAM prices fluctuate, when it's cheap, buy as much as you can.

#143 What Does Adobe Photoshop Offer?

With Adobe Photoshop, you take charge of what you want to do and how to go about doing it. To move quickly within Photoshop, familiarize yourself with the shortcut tools as they can save time and keystrokes. Next is a taste of what you can expect to accomplish:

- Various sized brushes that may be used in "painting"
- Drawing freehand with the Pen tool.
- Generate backgrounds with the Pattern Maker
- Unlimited layering capability
- Styles that allow the use of multiple effects
- Special effect filter for being "creative"
- Color correction capabilities
- A "healing brush" that can correct flaws while keeping the original look.
- Masking to hide elements

- Easy to use print function

- Protection in the form of a Watermark

- Cropping that preserves perspective

- Better blending through transparency controls

- A vector output for various shapes and text

- Animations from layered files—instantly

- Image maps, rollover and animations managed through a special palette

- You can paint, touch-up, composite, and draw with their unique toolset.

- Inspect before you open file capabilities

- Multiple do or undo displayed on a history palette

- A workspace that is customizable

- You can customize any tool

- Keep colors consistent with the management controls.

- Control dot gain

- If your colors are not "safe" Photoshop will tell you before printing.

#144 What Can I Do with a Low-End Program?

Low-end programs lack the punch that a more extensive program might have, but you still may be able to have your digital photo needs fulfilled. Basic trial or introductory software programs and even those that come with your digital camera will allow you to transfer images from the camera and may even offer a few other nice-to-have capabilities.

The most important things to look for in a low-end program are the features everyone will want to use most, such as resizing, red-eye reduction, simple color correction, and cropping. With these four items, you can tweak (not globally) or change most images to more acceptable ones. Other features like fancy borders, calendar tools, and text are alright, but you usually will need a beefier program.

The software package that comes with Canon, Nikon, and Kodak cameras is fine for making these small adjustments. If, however, your profession demands that you completely change the look of a picture, you will need a more powerful program like Photoshop or PhotoSuite.

Each program, even low-end ones, has different levels offered at a premium price. They will give you enough to get by, but you'll have to pay if you want the full package.

Look for free upgrades on the Internet for your low-end programs. As the bugs are worked out, the newer upgrade will function better than the old version. As your skills improve, you will want a better manipulation tool to cater to your every whim.

Chapter 14

Photoshop

#145 What Can't You Do with Photoshop?

Adobe Photoshop is by far the most popular software tool for manipulating images and that's why we're devoting an entire chapter just to scratch the surface of what it can do. In this chapter, you will learn how to retouch images, how to remove blemishes, how to remove scratches, how to sharpen an image, and how to blur an image. You'll learn how to reduce red eye, how to soften an image, how to add or remove something in an image, and how to change an image's background. The chapter will also cover how to crop an image, how to rotate an image, how to use the Clone tool, how to use the Dodge and Burn tools, how to use the paintbrushes, and how to add distortion. Various filters, such as the Displace filter, the Pinch filter, the Ripple filter, the Shear filter, the Twirl filter, and the Zigzag filter will be studied as well. Finally, you'll also learn how to do special effects, how to add text, and how to use text correctly. For further information on Photoshop, check out one of the many books on that program.

#146 How to Retouch Images

This solution works hand in hand with several others. Anytime you are manipulating an image, you are essentially retouching it. You may use several editing tools to retouch an image that you feel needs some attention.

For instance, you can use the *Smudge* tool to smear colors from a pristine area of the image to bare spots or other areas. You can smear the paint as far as you want, just as though the paint was still wet. This is one of the tools you'll use quite often.

The *Blur* tool, which looks like a water drop, can smooth pixels. This tool will blur the edges between colors so that the colors blend together.

The *Sharpen* tool, which resembles a sharp, narrow triangle, is used to rebuild textures. It also increases the amount of contrast between colors and builds up edges.

The *Blur* and *Sharpen* tools are known as the Focus tools. The Blur tool will soften transitions. When using the Sharpen tool, be careful to use it sparingly as it can make an image grainy.

The *Dodge* tool (not the automobile), which resembles a circle on the end of a stick, is used to lighten an area in your image evenly. The *Burn* tool, which looks like a hand in the shape of an O, can darken a portion of your image.

The *Sponge* tool is designed for use in full-color images. When working on a color image, this tool increases or decreases the color saturation. Increasing saturation makes the colors more vibrant while decreasing the saturation makes the colors drab looking. The Dodge, Burn, and Sponge tools are all considered Toning tools, meaning that they change the colors in an image.

Most of these tools should be used sparingly to achieve subtle effects in the digital image. If you change the image enough that someone can tell that you doctored the shot, you've gone too far. The trick is to enhance it slightly without calling attention to the fact.

#147 How to Remove Blemishes

No one is perfect and sometimes slight imperfections may need to be eliminated from a digital image. In the past, artists used to paint over an image's offending marks. Today we do the same thing electronically with Photoshop.

The Smudge tool is a great way to eliminate scars and wrinkles by pushing color from one portion of your image to another. When you drag with this tool, Photoshop grabs the color that's underneath your cursor and smears it in the direction of your drag.

We find it easier to enlarge the image so we have more control over our smudging. Working with a tiny area is too hard on the eyes and difficult to accurately correct.

Retouching with the Smudge tool is great, but be careful not to overuse it. With excessive use of this tool, you can create an image that doesn't look at all natural or real. You can use other editing tools to enhance your image and eliminate blemishes, but we feel the Smudge tool is an excellent choice.

#148 How to Remove Scratches

Sometimes we can scratch a photo and the only way to remove it is to blur the offending scar on the image. Photoshop does a great job of doing this with the Dust and Scratch removal selection.

In Photoshop, open your image and select the *Filter* menu. Go down to *Noise* and follow the arrow to *Dust and Scratches*. Position the connection tool box over the scratch and adjust the size of the image in the tiny box by clicking on the + or − square, anywhere from 6 to 800 percent.

Move the slider bar under *Radius* anywhere from 1 to 100 pixels and notice the change on the screen. In the same manner, the *Threshold* slider can also be adjusted from 0 to 255 levels. If *Preview* is checked, you can watch the changes occur.

Other tools in Photoshop like the *Clone* tool will also remove scratches. With this, you can copy the pixels from one area with no scratches and repair the other.

#149 How to Sharpen an Image

For whatever reason, sometimes you're not quite satisfied with your digital images. Perhaps you would like to make it a little sharper for printing.

For optimal sharpness, set your camera to its manual mode. Be sure to use the lowest compression and the highest resolution available for your camera. These are usually defined as an UltraFine or Fine mode. If your camera allows you, be sure to set your lens to its sharpest f-stop, which is generally two or three f-stops smaller than wide open (F5.6 or F8).

Setting your lens to the smallest f-stop will increase your overall depth of field, but the sharpness of an image will be somewhat reduced. Also, if your camera allows you, choose the highest possible shutter speed, such as 1/1000 or 1/500, and use a tripod.

When using a tripod, use a cable release that will prevent you from actually touching the camera. If a cable release is not available, the self-timer can accomplish the same thing. Focus is critical for utilizing your depth of field effectively. Additional sharpness can be added in editing, but if you can capture the image this way, it will look better.

If, in spite of all your efforts while taking your picture, your image needs additional sharpening, it's time to have some fun by editing the image. You can use the *Unsharp Mask*, which allows you to manually determine the amount of sharpness you desire. The *Sharpen* option makes the image a little sharper, while the *Sharpen More* option makes the image somewhat sharper at the price of adding grain. If you continue to click *Sharpen More*, eventually you won't be able to sharpen any further. Basically you've reached a stopping point. Avoid this problem by trying to shoot the picture as sharply as possible in the first place.

#150 How to Blur an Image

Without corrective lenses, most of us see the world through the *Blur* tool. But times will occur when a slight blur can add depth to the image and enhance the result.

The Blur tool blurs the edges between colors so that the colors blend together (they could have called it "blend.") To blur is to reduce the contrast between pixels that form edges in an image, softening it. Just as the Blur tool softens transitions, the Sharpen tool firms the transitions back up.

You can adjust the impact of the both the Blur and Sharpen tools by changing the *Pressure* setting in the *Options* bar. Most people that work with these Focus tools set the Pressure to about 60 percent for Blur and 30 percent for Sharpen. As with most other editing tools, be careful not to be excessive with the use of the Blur tool unless you're looking for a certain special effect, or just hope that everyone has really great eyesight.

#151 How to Reduce Red Eye

The best way to reduce red eye is before it occurs, but if you have an image with "devil eyes," it can be corrected. With Photoshop, you have all the tools needed to change the colors from red to the original hue. You can use a couple different methods.

The following method may not be the fastest way, but it keeps the structure of the pupil and the white light reflexes in the eye intact. Open the *Channel* palette and look for the best pupil (in this case, the darkest). Most likely it will be the *green* channel. Use the *Elliptical Marquee* tool from the toolbox to select one of the pupils. Hold down the *Shift* key to select the second pupil. With the Elliptical Marquee tool chosen, select *Anti-aliased* in the *Marquee Options* palette to define a smooth edge. Enter value **1** for the *Feather Radius* value to soften the edges of the selection. Copy the selected pupils when you are in the green channel only.

With the selections still active, click the *red* channel and choose *Edit > Paste Into* from the top Main menu of Photoshop. Copy the "good" pupil from the green channel into the "bad" one in the red channel. You now want to activate the blue channel and repeat the command *Paste Into*. Click the *RGB*-channel. This should work just fine; the other option isn't as accurate, but you see results faster.

The other method is to fire up your paintbrush, set it to a nice green, lower the opacity, and paint over the red using your Zoom tool. Green, for these purposes, is opposite red on the color wheel, so it's the complementary color. They will simply cancel each other out. This method will work for any version. You'll just have to mess with the opacity, depending on how red the eye is.

The *Cloning* tool can also be used to eliminate the red eye. Select a sample of the actual color of the eye. By using your Cloning tool, you can copy the true color of the eye over the red area and gradually blend to eliminate the red altogether.

#152 How to Soften an Image

You're not normally going to try to soften an image while making an exposure unless you intentionally use a filter over the lens to create a soft image, such as in a portrait or when photographing a model or a child. The softening effect is usually applied in editing.

With your image editor software, you'll have several choices. The Blur option makes the image just slightly blurry. The *Blur More* option will make the image a great deal more blurry. The *Gaussian Blur*, a counterpart of the Unsharp Mask, lets you determine exactly how much blurring you desire. Using the *Zoom Blur* makes the image grow or shrink, similar to a zoom lens. If you desire a streaky effect to indicate fast movement, try using the *Motion Blur*. Our best advice is to play around with these filters to see which works best in your specific situation.

#153 How to Remove Something from an Image

Since we are never satisfied with what we have, we constantly want to change it. It's really not difficult to remove something from an image, but some items will require more time, effort, and expertise to remove.

You may want to remove an individual from a group picture after being told that the person really shouldn't have been in the picture. You may have a tree or pole in the background directly behind someone and it appears as though it's growing out of the top of his or her head.

Using your image editor, you can simply select your *Rubber Stamp* or Clone tool. Whenever possible, enlarge your image so that you'll have a better look at the section you're changing. You'll want to select a portion of the image that you'd like to copy to place over the part of the image you want to remove.

Since you're using Photoshop, hold down the *Alt* key while clicking in that portion of the image. Select an area of the background that's near the area to be removed or use a generic object that you can paint over the unwanted portion of the image. Be sure to choose a brush size that will allow you to paint over the object in strokes. You can now add the replacement area over the unwanted part of your image.

We mentioned that this is not really that difficult, but like anything else that's new, the first few tries will take the longest as you learn how to perform this task. It's great to have the tools available to remove something from your original image. The "alt" key allows you to select or register the effect in Photoshop. Luckily, if you forget, it will tell you to press "alt" first.

At the same time, if you find you need to go through this procedure often, it will make you more aware to try and eliminate anything unnecessary while you're composing your shot and carefully reviewing the image in your camera.

#154 How to Add Something to an Image

The opposite of the last solution, you now must add something to the photo that wasn't there originally. This may involve adding a layer to your Photoshop document. Using layers, the process of addition becomes easier without destroying what was originally there.

We had a situation where someone missed a group photo and it was our dubious honor to add that person to the original shot. This is far more difficult that removing something because you have so many factors involved.

A shot of another person can easily fit in an old photograph, but adding something to an existing image consists of more than just inserting it. The addition should closely match the look of the old image. That means the lighting should be the same, so set your camera at the same ISO rate, and the person should be photographed from the same

Figure 14-1

Version 1 with something missing

focal point. Once you have matched the lighting, speed, and size of the person, the next step is the insertion process.

You've seen this adding process poorly done when someone takes an old photograph of Aunt Gertrude and blatantly sticks it on the body of Uncle Ralph. It's obvious that the two images don't match, and our job is to make them look as if they were taken at the same time. With a little bit of blending, an appendage can match the rest of the body.

To accomplish this, open the image you want to add to the old shot. Using the *Lasso* tool, trace around the outline of the person, expanding the image if necessary to see all the nuances. The *Magic Wand* tool may also be used if you want the entire person and the background is neutral; one keystroke does it all.

Select the *Move* icon and drag the person from the new photo over to the old one. When you release the mouse, he or she will drop into place. This is why it's important to light and size the addition correctly because it will save you time and aggravation in the transfer process. Figure 14-1 shows the old image and Figure 14-2 shows how the addition of the new person looking natural.

#155 How to Change the Background

For whatever reason, sometimes the background in your digital image isn't what you want, so a change is necessary. This can be accomplished in Photoshop in two different ways, so select the one that works for you.

Figure 14-2

Version 2 with the new photo added

#155

Open your image in Photoshop and select the Magic Wand icon. Pick a spot anywhere in the background of the photograph and click on it. The elusive dotted lines appear and most of your background should be selected. If the entire background is not highlighted, proceed to the next step; then repeat the process with the other section.

Once the background is highlighted, press Delete. This will essentially delete the background, leaving you with a checkerboard pattern, which is the absence of a background, or the Alpha channel. You could conceivably key or superimpose your subject over any background now.

If you desire a solid color background, select *Fill* under the *Edit* menu. You are now prompted to select a color and that becomes your new background. We do this often if we want to change the color of the sky in an image. We take out the "gray" and replace it with "blue." If you just want the star of your photo over a different background that isn't a color, open up that background image, select it with the Magic Wand, and choose Move. Now paste the new background over the vacated old one. Note that if the Magic Wand doesn't select enough of the background when you click it, while holding down Shift, keep selecting different areas with the Magic Wand until all of the background has been selected.

If you want your subject over a different existing background, the other option is to use the Magic Wand or Lasso and select the subject. Choose Move, move the object to another image containing the background you want, and paste it there.

Whether you move the subject from one background to another, or change the background behind the subject, it's your call. In very little time you will have this process mastered and you can flawlessly convert your images.

#156 How to Crop an Image

Cropping is the term used for cutting out a portion of the image you don't need. Consequently, you are making the original image smaller by removing a portion, but your new cropped image is actually enlarged.

You can use the *Crop* command to select part of an image and discard the rest or you can crop an image using the cropping tool in the toolbox. When you use the Crop command, you determine the area you want to save with the rectangular marquee tool. The advantage of using the Crop command is that you can rotate and resample the area as you crop.

To crop an image using the Crop command, double-click the marquee in the toolbox and choose *Rectangle* from the *Shape* menu in the Marquee Options palette. Be sure the Feather option is set to zero pixels. Select the part of the image you want to use, and then choose Crop from the Edit menu.

The *Crop* tool includes options that allow you to define the height-to-width ratio for the *Cropping Marquee* and the *Cropping Resolution*. Use the Crop tool to select part of an image and discard the rest. To use this tool, click the Crop tool in the toolbox. Drag to select the part of the image you want to use.

When you release the mouse button, the selected area will appear with four handles. Move the pointer inside the selected area, the pointer will turn into scissors, and then click the mouse button. At this point, the cropping has been completed.

#157 How to Rotate an Image

How often have you tried to scan an image in a hurry only to later find that the world is slightly askew? You can rotate an image to change its orientation or to simply straighten a crooked photo.

Typically, you'll be given the option of rotating your image in 90-degree increments, either clockwise, counterclockwise, or as much as 180 degrees. If you choose to rotate an image other than in 90-degree increments, your image editor will probably allow you to choose the *Arbitrary* command or something similar.

Arbitrary allows you to specify the amount of rotation and not be limited to a 90-degree change. There will be a type of dialog box that enables you to type in the amount of rotation you desire. Type in the number and it rotates it that much. Use + or − numbers to rotate left or right.

In PhotoSuite, if you choose something other than the 90-degree rotation elements, a clockwise and counterclockwise arrow is displayed. By clicking on these arrows, the image can be adjusted slightly.

Often you may not realize than an image needs to be rotated until you try to add a border or crop it in some way. The telltale pieces of the image outside of the dotted square remind you that everything may not be as straight as you once thought. These slight imperfections may be adjusted by using the Arbitrary or arrow commands, but sometimes just cropping out minor imperfections is easier.

In addition to rotating an image, you can also flip it to provide a mirror image. If you have a photo where somebody appears to be leaving the image area, you can flip it to make them appear to be entering the photo. You may also combine a flip and a rotation to end up with an image that is far different from the source. Just remember that a flip involves a mirror image and that will reverse any text in the picture. No one likes to read a backwards newspaper or T-shirt.

#158 How to Use the Clone Tool

This is the only type of cloning you can do that's legal and ethical. Basically, a clone is an exact reproduction of something, a duplicate that matches in every way. When you make a copy of a digital print, it essentially is a clone because it is an exact, digital duplicate. A copy of a 35mm photo is just that, a copy. This copy does not match the original exactly because there could be slight changes in hue, saturation, and so on. The quality is also slightly less in a copy, not so in a clone.

The Clone tool options take a sample of the entire image, which you can then apply or paint over another image. Each stroke of the tool paints on more of the sampled image, starting at the point where you took your first sample. The aligned Clone option applies a sampled image continuously, regardless of how many times you stop and resume painting. This option is especially useful when you want to use different sized brushes to paint an image. You can also use the aligned Clone option for painting two halves of an image on either side of another image. When using aligned clone it allows different choices in brushes without you having to stop and reset everything for end brush stroke.

The nonaligned Clone option applies a sampled image from the initial sampling point each time you stop and resume painting. Nonaligned clone makes you reset everything each time you select a different brush. Aligned as the name implies, means everything is "aligned" for you. Nonaligned is more random where you are "sketching" your clone freehand, rather than "drawing" more formally. Because the Rubber Stamp tool samples the entire image, this Clone option is useful when applying multiple copies of part of an image.

#159 How to Use the Dodge and Burn Tools

The Dodge and Burn tools are based on the traditional photographer's technique of increasing the amount of exposure given to a specific area on a finished print. The photographer would hold back light during an exposure to lighten an area on the print (dodge) or increase the exposure to darken areas of the print (burn). This dealt with a negative, so it is the opposite of what you would assume.

To choose options for the Dodge and Burn tools, double-click the tool to display the *Toning Tools Option* palette. You'll then make your selection to dodge or burn from the Tool menu. You can then select a mode that will limit the changes to a specific part of the image.

Choose *Shadows* to alter the dark portions of the image or select *Highlights* to change or modify only the light areas. You can also select the *Midtones* mode (sounds like a lounge act) to change only the middle range of colors in your image. Simply drag the slider in the Options palette to set the exposure and you're finished. Figure 14-3 illustrates the original image and Figure 14-4 shows what happens when dodging is applied. Figure 14-5 is an example of a burn applied to an image.

#160 How to Use the Paintbrushes

This is the easiest kind of paintbrush to use without the mess. The *Paintbrush* tool creates soft strokes that are not as hard-edged as the lines drawn with the *Pencil* tool and not as soft as the strokes painted with the *Airbrush* tool.

To choose options for the Paintbrush tool, double-click the Paintbrush tool in the toolbox to display the *Paintbrush Options* palette. Choose a mode from the menu on the left of the palette. Drag the slider to set the opacity. Click the *Fade* option to set a fade-out rate. You can also click *Wet Edges* to paint with a watercolor effect. With this option selected, the paint builds up along the edges of the brushstroke.

Figure 14-3

The original
face

Figure 14-4

Now she is
dodging the
issue. Her flash is
much lighter.

Figure 14-5

That really *burned* her up.

The brushes you use for the painting tools appear in the *Brushes* palette. Round brush shapes for painting are available in several sizes. Adobe Photoshop allows you to save the brush settings for each painting tool, so you can select a different default brush for each tool. The Brushes palette also contains commands for creating and deleting brushes, defining brush options, and saving and loading sets of brushes. Use the Brushes palette to choose a brush shape for any painting tool.

To choose a brush shape, click the tool you want to use in the toolbox. You'll then want to choose *Palettes* > *Show Brushes* from the *Window* menu. The Brushes palette appears and the brush for the current tool is selected. You can now click any brush shape you want to use.

Brushes that are too large to fit in a square on the palette are shown with a number displayed under the brush preview. This number indicates the diameter of the brush in pixels.

#161 How to Add Distortion

Times may occur when you want to add distortion to your digital image. The only way to effectively achieve this is by using a software program, such as Adobe Photoshop. The series of *Distort* filters produces a geometrical distortion of an image, depending on the look you're after.

In the next several solutions, various types of distortion attributes will be explained. Depending on the specific effect you require, the final result could look far different than your original.

#162 How to Use the Displace Filter

The *Displace* filter uses a second image (called a displacement map) to determine how to distort the selection. The filter reads a color value from the displacement map and uses the value to displace the selection. A value of 0 is maximum negative displacement, and a value of 225 is the maximum positive displacement. A gray value of 128 produces no displacement. Unless you have a specific number in mind, try several different number combinations to see what best suits your needs.

#163 How to Use the Pinch Filter

The *Pinch* filter in the Distort submenu squeezes a selection together. It's almost as if you are grabbing a portion of the image and pinching it together, causing a distortion.

To shift a selection toward its center, enter a positive value in the Pinch dialog box. To shift a selection outward, enter a negative value. Values can range from +100 percent to −100 percent. The dialog box will show you the Pinch pattern produced by the value.

#164 How to Use the Ripple Filter

As the name ripple suggests, the *Ripple* filter produces an undulating pattern on a selection. To use the Ripple filter, choose Distort and then Ripple from the *Filter* menu, causing the Ripple dialog box to appear. Enter a value in the *Amount* box for the magnitude of the ripples.

Values can range from -199 to +199. Click *Small*, *Medium,* or *Large* to set the ripple frequency. You can use the feathering to mute the edges of the ripple where the selection blends into the background.

The *Wave* filter works much like the Ripple filter but gives you more control over the effect.

The *Pond Ripples* option displaces pixels to the upper left or lower right. The *Out from Center* option displays pixels toward or away from the center of the selection. The *Around Center* option rotates pixels around the center.

#165 How to Use the Shear Filter

The *Shear* filter distorts an image along a curve you specify. To use the Shear filter, choose Distort and then Shear from the Filter menu and the Shear dialog box appears. Drag the line in the box to form a curve that indicates how you want the image to be distorted. You can adjust any point along the curve. Click *Reset* to return the curve to a straight line. Select an option to determine how areas of the image left undefined by the shear are treated.

#166 How to Use the Twirl Filter

The *Twirl* filter in the Distort submenu rotates a selection more sharply in the center than at the edges, making a twirl effect. To use this filter, enter an *Angle* value in the Twirl filter dialog box. Values can range from 999 to -999. The box to the side of this value shows you the twirl pattern produced by the value.

#167 How to Use the Zigzag Filter

The *Zigzag* filter distorts a selection radially, depending on the radius of the pixels in your selection. To use the Zigzag filter, choose Distort > Zigzag from the Filter menu and the Zigzag dialog box appears.

Enter a value in the *Amount* box for the magnitude of distortion. The values can range from -100 to +100. The box on the side shows you the Zigzag pattern produced by the value. Enter a value in the *Ridges* box to set the number of direction reversals of the zigzag, from the center of the selection to the edges. Values here can range from 1 to 20. You'll also need to select how to displace the pixels.

#168 How to Do Special Effects

Sometimes you're going to feel like experimenting with the special effects or you've been asked to do something creative with an image. With Photoshop, you have all the tools you can imagine, and more. So many ways exist for creating special effects from an ordinary image that you may want to purchase a Photoshop user guide that corresponds with the version you're using.

The first thing you'll need to do is open an image and decide whether you want to distort the whole image or just a portion. We'll give you just a sample of some of the tools you can use to create those special effects. The *Warp* tool pushes the pixels forward under your brush as you drag, creating a stretched look. This tool will give you a taffy-like appearance.

The *Twirl* tool rotates the pixels clockwise under your brush as you either drag or hold down the mouse. Guess what the *Twirl Counterclockwise* tool does? Exactly, it rotates the pixels in a counterclockwise direction.

The *Pucker* tool moves the pixels toward the center of your brush as you hold down the mouse, giving the image a pinched look. The *Bloat* tool is the opposite of the *Pucker* tool. It moves pixels away from the center, creating a spherical effect.

The *Shift Pixels* tool shifts the pixels to where you move the brush in that direction. The *Reflection* tool copies pixels to an area perpendicular from their original spot only in a perpendicular direction.

After you've altered your image by using one or more of the special effect tools, you'll need to be sure to click OK. Up to this point, Photoshop has just been displaying a proxy of the image. Consider it a temporary preview. If these effects are what you really want applied to your image, you must click OK and exit the dialog box.

#169 How to Add Text

Depending on the version of Photoshop you're using, the *Adding Text* option may vary somewhat. For the discussion in this area, we'll be using the *Text* options for Photoshop 6 even though some of you may have a newer version. For those of you with a newer version, forgive us. We're just trying to hit a happy medium for our readers and maybe someone nice will send us version 7.

Photoshop 6 changes the configuration of the Type tools. What were four separate tools residing in the toolbox now consist of one tool in the toolbox with four options in the *Options* bar. The regular *Type* tool icon looks like a big letter *T*, and the keyboard shortcut is the letter T also. The four options in the Options bar consist of creating a text layer, a mask or selection, and horizontal and vertical orientation.

To type a few letters in Photoshop, select the Type tool and click inside the image anywhere you want. Photoshop positions the text at the spot you click, but you can move the text anywhere you choose after you create it.

With the new and improved method of adding text, you'll see a blinking cursor (insertion marker) that you may have seen when working in other programs. After the insertion marker appears, you can enter your text. This "click and type" method results in *point text* or *box text* (also referred to as paragraph text).

Point text is type created from a single point and is free-floating with each line being independent from one another. This works well for a word or a short line of text.

Box text is text created in a box that flows according to its dimensions. Box text is best suited for large amounts of type. If you want your text to automatically wrap with the boundary or you want to justify your text, box text is the way to go. While typing your text, you can utilize the *Copy*, *Cut*, *Paste,* and *Undo* commands under the Edit menu, just like in a word processing program. Of course, all your normal options, such as selecting font size and style, color, type justification, and alignment, as well as other options, are all available.

#**170** How to Use Text Correctly

Knowing how to add text to your digital image is the first part of the battle, but knowing how to use it correctly is even more important. Choosing the wrong font style, cramming too much information on the image, or improper justification are three of the areas we'll discuss in this solution.

Pick a font style that suits your digital image. You have hundreds of options, but most are very elaborate and will not work well with a photograph. Unless you are after a specific special effect, using the font Monkey will just give you various sizes and shapes of monkeys.

Instead, choose an easily readable font like Ariel, Times Roman, or something along those lines. Creepy is a great font if you're doing a horror still, but not much good anywhere else.

When adding text, make the characters as bold and as dark as possible to contrast from the image beneath it. You also have the option of changing the transparency, but anything less than 50 percent will be distracting to the eye. Choose a dark font over a light image and the opposite over a dark image. Space the letters accordingly (kerning), and apply a drop shadow, outline, or glow to further separate the text from the photo.

Keep all your text to a minimum since too many words will take away from the impact of the image. Just say what you must in as few words as possible and let the photo speak for itself. If two lines work better than one, use them. The smaller the type, the more difficult it will be to read. Look at ads in magazines and see how they incorporate text and photos. If the text is too light or dark, the ad will be difficult to read and sales will be lost.

Justification is also misused. Ads have a tendency to use centered text, because it draws the eye faster. It is also more difficult to read because the eye must scan to the center of the image, read it, and then scan back to the center of the next line. It is more time consuming to read, but only in milliseconds.

If you have a lot of text (several lines), left-justify it just like you would see in a book. This is the easiest format to read and more information may be crammed in. Right justification is the hardest to read and is only used when the image warrants that type of positioning.

#170

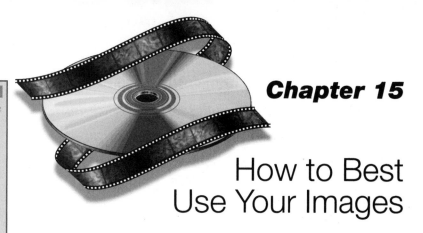

How to Best Use Your Images

#171 How to Best Use Your Images

This chapter will talk about getting your images into the hands of other people and the best ways for doing so. They include how to display your images on a web site, how to send e-mail photos, how to lessen the upload time, and how to use progressive scan. The chapter will also cover how to create slide show presentations, how to project digital images, how to use PowerPoint, how to create newsletter-ready or newspaper-ready photos, and how to personalize special occasion graphics.

#172 How to Display Images on a Web Site

When designing a web page in HTML, Dreamweaver, or any of a number of programs, photos always make the site look more appealing. By displaying the images as thumbnails, the user can click on them to see a larger version of the photo.

Digital images are great for web sites because even the inexpensive camera can produce more resolution than is really needed. Nice, clear, and crisp images are attractive on a web site, but they shouldn't take forever to download. You need to have your images appear quickly to keep your visitor interested because none of us like to wait.

Pay particular attention to the number and size of your page's graphics. Most people feel that the individual images should be 50KB or less and all the images of your page should not exceed 100KB.

Use only the important part of your image and crop anything that doesn't add to the overall impact. If cropping won't allow you to get your picture down to reasonable pixel dimensions, resize your image. Most image editors show the size of the image in kilobytes or megabytes at the bottom of the screen.

In Photoshop, the *Image Size* box displays the final dimensions before you apply the size modifications. A good way to reduce the file size of an image for a web page is by using the JPEG compression option available in your image editor. JPEG discards some of the information, resulting in the picture not being quite as sharp as the original, but for a web page you'll never notice the difference. JPEG is best for full-color photographic images, as opposed to charts, graphs, line art, or text.

Compressing an image for the Web with *graphics interchange format* (GIF) is not ideal for photographs because GIF only uses 256 different colors. If you happen to have an image with just a few colors, GIF can produce even smaller file sizes than *Joint Photographic Experts Group* (JPEG). The GIF format is best suited for line art and text. Both JPEG and GIF can be used on the Web, but just be sure to consider what you're displaying and the best method to use.

The idea is to display an image on the web page that will peak the viewer's interest. Thumbnails take up little space and load quickly. The whole idea is to get the viewer to the site, and then he or she can see a larger version of the image when they click the thumbnail.

#173 How to E-mail Photos

It's extremely easy to send images over the Internet via e-mail. Thanks to your digital camera, you have images that you can easily share with family, friends, and coworkers. You have the option of sending your pictures in a GIF or JPEG format, although GIF is more suitable for line art and text as opposed to photographs. JPEG works best when e-mailing color images.

The other factor when sending photos via e-mail is the size of the image. By size, we are not referring to a 4 × 6 or an 8 × 10, but the number of kilobytes or megabytes. The sharper the resolution, the larger the file size. The number of pixels determines this size or the *dots per inch* (dpi) of the image. A 1,200 dpi image may be over 45MB and will take hours to upload and download on a phone modem, even at 56KB. However, we will go into more detail on resizing images in a subsequent solution.

When you're ready to e-mail your image, address the e-mail to your recipient. If you have a mailing list already set up, you can send your images to everyone on your list at one time. As with any other e-mail message, you can include any text that you want to send along with your picture. Some people tend to make these messages humorous depending on the subject and person who will be receiving the images. Often we tend to get so creative with our text message that we forget to send along the attached file with the pictures. Don't be concerned; this happens all the time.

With different e-mail programs, your commands will vary slightly. When using AOL, click the Attachments button on the bottom of the message dialog box. With Microsoft Outlook, choose Insert > File and with Outlook Express, choose Insert > File Attachment. Click Send or OK to mail your message. If you want to make sure everything went according to plan, you can go to your Sent Items file and check.

One minor flaw with a JPEG image is that each time it opens, the file recompresses. Opening a JPEG the first time is fine, but if you open the same file numerous times, the file compresses and uncompresses each time. Most often we will never notice anything, but if sending critical high-quality work via e-mail, keep this in mind. Other methods like Targa, the *tagged image file format* (TIFF), or even Adobe Photoshop files will not go through this compression process when opened and closed, but the files do take up more space.

We've also been asked if an image sent numerous times to many different people loses any image quality. The answer is absolutely not! It's not like copying or scanning a traditional picture. This is the digital age and that makes all the difference.

#174 How to Lessen the Upload Time

It gets very frustrating waiting for your web image to upload. The faster your connection speed, the less time it takes, but it usually will still take some time. What can you do to speed up this process so do don't age as quickly during the wait?

The best thing you can do is to keep your files as small as possible. An image that is 1MB will take three times longer to upload than a picture that's 250KB. Photoshop (and other software programs) will allow you to change the image size in resolution as well as format. Once you make your change, at the bottom of the screen the program will tell you how long (in minutes and seconds) it should take your image to load with a 28.8 or 56KB modem. Depending on the Internet connection you may have, the time limit will vary and you can dial in what you have connection-wise and get an accurate approximation of your wait.

When we are uploading JPEGs for a web page, we will always have thumbnails (discussed earlier) on the web page itself, but the full-size images also need to be available for the user to see if he or she wants.

Prepare your image before uploading and make the file size as small as possible; it doesn't matter what your connection speed. If it takes you five seconds to upload because you have a high-speed (expensive) connection, it may still take the users hours to download images with their antique connection.

If you have a high-quality 1,200 dpi color image saved as a JPEG, convert it to a lesser size JPEG for the Internet. In a software program, choose *Save As* or *Save for Web* to get a selection of options. Instead of *High* or *Medium*, choose *Low* as the JPEG file size. You still have three options in *Low* (1, 2, or 3). Try saving your image in each one of these values in *Low* and notice the difference in loading time.

Along the same lines, instead of having a full size 8 × 10 image whose quality will never be seen on a computer screen, decrease the photo to 5 × 7 or 4 × 6. If viewers want more detail or a larger image, they can always enlarge it and zoom in on their end, saving everyone time. The idea is to get your file as small as possible, lessening the upload and download times while still keeping some quality there.

#175 How to Use Progressive Scan

Progressive scan is a real time-saver when downloading images. Instead of waiting and staring at a blank screen hoping for the image to appear, the viewer will see it build, giving him or her something to look at during the waiting process.

What progressive scan does is slowly scan the image onto the screen line by line. As the picture is downloading, some of it is held in a buffer so it may be partially displayed on the screen as the information is received.

This option can be selected in software programs when you choose Save for Web. Progressive scan takes no more or less time for the image to load, but the user will see that something is happening instead of wondering if his or her computer has locked up. The viewer may have clicked the wrong thumbnail and instead of waiting for the incorrect image to load, the progressive scan shows them, bit by bit, that what they're going to get may not be what they wanted. Thus, they can quit the process earlier.

Most people prefer this type of download, mainly because they can see that "something is happening." Living in an impatient society, people want things immediately and the progressive download is one small way of making that appear to happen faster. At least we try to do what we can.

#176 How to Create Slide Show Presentations

It's probably been some time since a friend, relative, or colleague has suggested that you take a look at his or her slide presentation, especially when he or she mentions the projector is set up, the screen is in place, and the slides are in the carousel ready to be shown.

We're way beyond that technology and to the point where we realize that digital pictures are great for computerized presentations. They can be produced quickly, contain the proper resolution, and will enhance your overall presentation. If this is new to anyone or you'd like to enhance your skills with this type of a presentation, you may want to borrow from the library or purchase a copy of *PowerPoint for Dummies*. Don't be insulted by the name; it's the content that counts.

In a business presentation, you can incorporate your company name or logo to each slide; add charts, graphs, and photos; and easily customize your presentation to different audiences. Creative and colorful borders can add to your presentation but should not compete with the contents of your slides. Your software contains wizards or templates that can make the slide presentation a much easier process.

PowerPoint is one of the best software applications for creating slide presentations, and incorporating your digital still images is as easy as clicking Import. Be careful not to try to add too much information to any one slide, as it becomes busy-looking and may be difficult to interpret. Some people prefer to add narration to the slide show using your software's recording capabilities. In any case, leave the material on the screen long enough for it to be digested without boring the viewer. A feature within PowerPoint called *Pack and Go* allows you to package your presentation for your audience, even though PowerPoint may not be installed on their computer.

#177 How to Project Digital Images

With the advent of better projection systems, a digital image may be displayed on the screen easily with very little setup time.

When 35mm slides were king, it took quite a while to set up a bulky slide projector and move it around the room so it could properly fill the screen. You also had to hope that the 12-hour life span of the bulb wasn't going to end during your presentation.

Digital *liquid crystal display* (LCD) projectors are now much smaller than the old three-gun video projectors and even more portable than their 35mm counterpart. The technology has improved enough that you will get a brighter picture, longer life from the lamp, a zoom control that will fill any screen from a shorter distance, and image reversibility for front-, rear-, or ceiling-mounted projection, all in something that can fit in your briefcase.

Video projectors are measured in lumens or brightness. The higher the number of lumens, the more intense the image. Newer models with 5,000 lumens can display an image in a room with all the lights on and still be easy on the eye. The days of viewing images in complete darkness and trying to take notes have passed.

The lamps or bulbs no longer burn out after only 12 hours of life. Instead, as they get older after hundreds if not thousands of hours, they will progressively dim. As the projected image gets darker and darker, you will know that the time to replace the lamp is near. This is far better than having a lamp go out in the middle of a presentation. Now at least you have some warning and may prepare.

We've seen projectors whose image could fill a 10-foot screen placed only 5 feet away. In cramped conference rooms, the presenter may now be in the front of the room, close to the projector, instead of hiding in a dark, back corner. With a push of a button, the image will fill almost any sized screen.

Eliminating any fear of what you may be walking into, digital projectors can display an image from in front of the screen, behind the screen for rear projection, or flipped for a ceiling mount. This is great for salespeople who never know what kind of environment they may have to cater to.

With the clarity of today's lenses, a low- to medium-resolution digital image will still look good onscreen. The projector will accept almost any source of input: a serial cable from a computer, *Universal Serial Bus* (USB), FireWire, *British Naval Connector* (BNC), Super VHS (S-VHS), RGB, or RCA video connections. This is pretty amazing from something that weighs only a few pounds yet can present your best work to the masses.

#**178** How to Use PowerPoint

If you had to pick one single thing that has changed the lives of salespeople and presenters, it would have to be PowerPoint. This incredible software program can display color photographs, charts, graphs, text, and even motion video, all from the confines of a computer.

PowerPoint has been around for quite some time and is usually loaded on any computer that has a office or business version of Microsoft (Apple also offers it). Set up much like any other computer program, you can build your presentation from scratch by selecting prebuilt items from the menus, or drawing and importing your own.

Animations may be added to still images and the computer will toggle between sources to simulate movement. Because PowerPoint is such a visual medium, a constant need exists for high-quality images to present to the public.

A program may be designed in PowerPoint, saved on the computer's hard drive, or even burned to a CD-ROM. The program can now be presented to the audience on a laptop computer for a one-to-one showing, or it can be connected to a video projector in order for the CEO to explain the company's profit and loss history. A CD-ROM may be mass duplicated and sent to everyone for display on their computers. However, a 700MB CD can display too many hours of images and diagrams for anyone's comfort zone.

Great books are available on how to specifically design a Power-Point program, which is very straightforward and easy to use. We taught ourselves how to use it in a short period of time with just instructions gathered from the Help menu.

One of the best features of PowerPoint is that you can build the program image by image, incorporating still photos, charts, and video. You can then view it as a slide show, checking out the timing of each segment. With a push of the spacebar, your program is now in presentation mode.

#179 How to Prepare Images for Display on a Computer

When preparing images for display on PowerPoint, or on any computer for that matter, remember that the aspect ratio (width to height) is not the same on a computer or TV screen as it is in real life. An 8 × 10 digital photo is too tall and not wide enough to fit on a computer screen.

We're used to holding a 4 × 6 image in our hands and seeing the entire picture; any size photo works. But when we try to show that same image on a computer screen, too much space is left around the image.

As an example, an 8 × 10 photograph is 8 units wide by 10 units tall (we know it's inches, but any measurement will do for this example). A computer monitor, much like a television screen, is 4 × 3, or four units wide by three units tall. If we enlarge the picture to fit this aspect ratio, we lose information on the top and bottom because the sides need to be wider.

If we stretch or make the image wider to fit our new screen dimensions, the picture distorts because we are stretching it unnaturally. Much like watching an old Cinemascope movie on TV, everything is squeezed together to make a roughly 16 × 9 (widescreen or high-definition) image fit on a 4 × 3 viewing medium. Something will get lost.

When you rent a movie in widescreen or letterbox, black bands can be seen at the top and bottom of the screen because the aspect ratio is different. You must do the same thing to your digital images to make them fit on the computer screen. Either you must have a border around the image or a colored background to fill up the space between your full image and the rest of the screen. Figure 15-1 illustrates the original image in all its glory. Figure 15-2 shows that same image sized to fit the computer screen. All of the information is still there; we just have a lot more area to fill.

The other options are to cut off the areas that won't fit on the screen, losing picture information, or expand the image to fit. If you choose the latter, you must enlarge the width and height in order to keep the proportions of the image accurate. If you stretch the width too much,

Figure 15-1

The original image

Figure 15-2

The same image sized to fit on a computer screen

Figure 15-3

The image is cropped to fit the computer screen. Information is lost.

everything looks flat and squashed. If the vertical is extended too much, that weight loss program was effective.

In the latter of these two methods, you will lose some visual information with the equal stretching being the least destructive. Figure 15-3 shows what happens to an image if you just crop the areas that don't fit.

Figure 15-4

Expanding the width and height makes a better computer image with less information lost.

Figure 15-4 shows how you can enlarge the width and height for a better looking photo.

#180 How to Add Motion to Your Still Images

Sometimes in a visual demonstration, you'd like a little movement in your digital stills to make them come to life. Using the magic of digital, you can make this a reality.

On a recent TV commercial, we had to add movement and action to numerous still photos of a housing development. We could have just left the still images on the screen without movement, but in a medium like television, people expect things to happen rather than just sit there.

In our case, we used a free plug-in offered by Avid when you purchase their Avid Xpress Digital Video (DV) nonlinear editing program. We know this a motion video program, but we needed our still photos to move. Using the *Pan and Zoom* plug-in, we could determine and position where we wanted all movement in the still photographs, just like a motion control camera does, this time without the camera.

You've seen this effect used in TV documentaries when a black and white photograph is shown. The camera zooms in on someone in the picture or pans left or right to show something else in the frame. In the old days, someone with a film or video camera had to set the picture on an easel, mount the camera on a tripod, and then fluidly zoom in or out to maneuver around the picture at a constant and steady pace.

Motion control cameras have made this easier because a computer performs perfect, fluid moves over and over without the possible shaking that a human camera operator would cause. The Pan and Zoom software does the same thing without the expense of the motion control camera.

Once the image is loaded in the computer, you select the type of move you want: zoom, pan, or tilt (or a combination of all three). By dragging the cursor in the path of your movement, the computer remembers the X (horizontal), the Y (vertical), and the Z (depth) parameters.

After you render this movement, hit the spacebar and a motion control camera moves over your digital image, panning, tilting, and zooming at any speed you determine. The greatest thing about this is that it's accurate, smooth, flawless, and it can happen over and over again. This movement adds interest to a still image because the viewer is being shown exactly want you want them to see in the photograph and when.

#181 How to Make Newsletter-Ready Photos

When creating a company or family newsletter, digital photos are a quick and easy way to get your images together and published. This is a great way to easily use your digital images.

You'll need to save your images at the highest resolution possible so that your local printer can provide you with the best possible pictures. If you intend to print this yourself on your own printer, you'll still get the best possible results when saving at a high resolution.

If your camera gives you the option of saving in a raw format or TIFF file, certainly do so. You won't be able to fit many images on your storage medium, but you'll be able to reproduce the best possible image for your newsletter. The reason for originating the picture in the highest resolution possible is because the quality will be lowered slightly when printed on paper. Photographic paper keeps the image sharper, however.

You can do any cropping or retouching using your image editor and save as a TIFF file. Insert the image into your newsletter using your desktop publishing program or give the image to your professional printer.

#182 How to Make Newspaper-Ready Photos

Larger newspapers have a staff of photographers that they send on an assignment they feel is newsworthy. Whether it's a groundbreaking event, a dignitary's visit, a news briefing by the mayor, or a photo to accompany an article in the local business section, they typically send their staff photographers.

Of course, human interest stories occur while traveling on business or a vacation. Possibly your local club has an event and the paper chose not to cover the story with a picture. If you've captured an image, approach the newspaper about their interest in publishing your pictures. Many local newspapers will accept prints or digital images, but if they receive a high-quality digital image that they don't need to improve or enhance, they're delighted. (If you send prints, they'll have to scan them anyway.)

Be sure to take your picture using the maximum resolution your digital camera has to offer. Feel free to correct for exposure and color, but don't do anything complex that would make it apparent that the photo has been altered. If a newspaper receives an image and it is obvious that significant changes have been made, they may be somewhat hesitant to accept and publish them. The less you need to manipulate the image, the better.

It's best not to worry about cropping the final image. The newspaper will have a better idea on what size will suit their needs, and it is more difficult to uncrop an image than the other way around. Just give them a loosely framed image and allow them to change it accordingly.

If the newspaper is willing to review your image, ask them if they prefer a floppy disk, a ZIP disk, or other media. If the newspaper agrees, ask for a photo credit to be included with the picture. If they're really impressed, they may want to have you do contract work for them, so be sure to include information on how you may be reached. Don't be bashful; the worst they can say is that they're not interested due to space constraints or other reasons.

Every newspaper photographer we've worked with uses a digital camera for shooting. The amount of savings in film stock and processing alone makes this an easy decision. Even *National Geographic* is slowly switching from Kodachrome slide film to an all-digital format.

#183 How to Personalize Special Occasion Graphics

It's always nice to receive an e-mail from a friend, relative, or coworker, but when an image is attached to the message, it somehow becomes special and we just can't wait to see what it might be (unless the attachment comes from a site Mom doesn't want us to look at).

This is especially true if a hint of what to expect is given in the subject line. When choosing what to call your subject, many people like to include the date, especially if they're sending a picture of a baby or a puppy, so you'll be able to easily determine when the picture was taken.

All image editors have a *text* tool that will allow you to add a certain amount of text to your photos. We find it's best to keep the text to a minimum, as it actually appears on the image area. After you've chosen your image editor's text tool, select the position where you want the text to appear as well as the text's color.

In most cases, you'll need to click and drag to create the area where the text will appear. Be sure to pick an appropriate color that will stand out but not detract from the photo. At this point, you'll have options as to the font size, style, and other special formatting such as *italic* or **bold**. Type your text in the box you've created and click OK when you're finished. When you are satisfied, hit the *Send* button and you're about to make somebody's day a little brighter.

Chapter 16

Seeing the Image

#184 How to See the Image in Its Best Light

Now that you have all these great images stored in some medium, it's time to get them into a form the entire world can see, and that's to get it on photo paper. This chapter will discuss the nuances of printing your favorite digital images, such as how to print an image, what size you should print to, how to make your prized images last almost forever by archiving, and how the different types of photo paper out there differ from each other. The chapter will also discuss how to use an inexpensive inkjet printer or a higher-quality laser printer, and how to choose the best type of printer to fit your needs. We'll also examine how to determine the speed of your printer, how to get enough memory to keep your printer from bogging down, how to keep the supplies and accessories from breaking you financially, how to determine the best printer size to fit in your space, how to decide how many *dots per inch* (DPI) are sufficient, how to use a laser printer to your advantage, and, lastly, how to use a scanner.

#185 How to Print an Image

One of the few drawbacks to digital cameras is that you don't get images printed on paper as part of the process. Of course, you can immediately see the results of each shot, but sometimes we like the feel of holding the photo in our hands and not just seeing it on a computer or *liquid crystal display* (LCD) screen. This is the time to physically print out the photo.

It's always a good idea to save your image before you print. The printing process is one of many tasks that can cause problems with your computer, such as locking up or, worse yet, crashing. Selecting a printer is only necessary if you're part of a network. Using a stand-alone computer and your printer, you'll simply need to select the paper size and the page orientation. Go to *File* and find your *Page Setup* box. Photoshop displays a preview of how your image will fit the paper. If the image is too large to fit on the page, you can reduce the image by using the *Image Size* command. To make the image fit, you can decrease the *Width* and *Height* values until the entire image will fit on the page.

The next step is to choose the correct printing paper. Photo paper comes in many qualities, gloss levels, and prices. Don't buy the inexpensive 200-page packs if you only intend to print out a few images occasionally. Archival characteristics have increased and a computer-printed image should hold its colors for up to 25 years if it's stored properly. Some printers will even allow you to select what brand of photo paper to use (HP does). Obviously, any paper but photo paper will degrade the printed image.

After you feel comfortable that the image will fit onto the paper size you've selected, go for it and hit the *Print* button. If the image is still too large for the page, Photoshop displays an error message warning you that your image will be cut off and will ask whether you want to continue or proceed. If you indicate no, the error message disappears, and you can resize the image to fit the page. If you indicate you want to print anyway, the Print dialog box will disappear. Usually, the image will now be borderless and extend to the edges of the paper.

If you feel certain that the image should fit on the paper but Photoshop insists that it won't, check your page orientation in your Page Setup dialog box. Photoshop will insist that your image is too large if your orientation (landscape or portrait) is not set properly.

If you have a quality printer and use good photo paper, your print should be quite acceptable. Fuji and Kodak are examples of good-quality paper.

#**186** What Is the Best Size to Print To?

Hopefully, in the process of selecting your digital camera, you give serious consideration to what you plan on using the camera for. Keep in mind that most megapixel cameras produce images suitable for 4 × 6 prints. If you make 5 × 7, 8 × 10, or larger prints, you would need to consider cameras with resolutions of at least 1600 × 1200 pixels.

If your main objective is to satisfy your boss as the "designated in-house photographer" responsible for capturing images for a web page or newsletter, you may choose a lower-end, less expensive digital camera. If you happen to fall into this category or anywhere close, a cheaper camera would be the right choice.

Now suppose your boss has you take a photo of everyone in your department for the company newsletter. Your boss likes the photo so much that he wants to have it enlarged to a 20 × 24 print and that it be matted and framed for the office lobby. The image capture capabilities of your digital camera are going to determine how large you're going to be able to print. We've discussed previously the many ways you can enhance an image, but many limitations exist, especially when it comes to image size and resolution and your ability to make large prints. Many people have purchased low-end digital cameras as their first step into the digital arena, but then realize they want to do more than what the camera is capable of doing.

But that's okay! You tried a low-end camera and liked it; now it's time to look at a higher-end digital camera that better suits your needs. Of course, you can keep your original camera as a backup or use it when you know you can get by with a particular sized finished image.

As for answering this solution's question, no "best" size exists. It depends on the end usage of the image. As mentioned earlier, storing or archiving photographs should be done in a smaller, more manageable size like 4 × 6. Any other larger size depends on the capabilities of the camera and what the client or end user wants.

#187 How Best to Archive Photos

In order for your digital images to last, you must find a safe way of archiving them so the ravages of time and a lack of equipment don't erase your memories. With compression capabilities such as the *Joint Photographic Experts Group* (JPEG), a digital image takes up much less space on your hard drive. This isn't to say that you won't want or need to archive your pictures, but there's really no purpose in taking up hard drive space, so you'll want to archive your images to a convenient type of storage. This storage media will also provide a backup in the event you have major problems with your computer.

How to archive your images is a personal preference and you have many options. You may choose to archive to a floppy disk, which is inexpensive, readily available, and usable by anyone with a computer. The drawback to using a floppy disk is that at 1.44MB, the floppy can't store many images.

If resolution isn't important, you can save the images from your image editor using quite a bit of compression. Keep in mind that all the data you squeeze out of your images using JPEG will be gone permanently. When saving to a floppy, save them to a PC-formatted floppy even if you're using a Macintosh. You'll be able to read the disk on a Mac or a Windows computer. Be sure to set the write-protect tab after saving on your floppy so you don't accidentally write over your archived files. Floppies are basically magnetic film in a plastic housing. They are inexpensive and will fail if used too much, placed near a magnetic field, or manhandled severely.

High-density disks such as Iomega Zip disks or Imitation SuperDisks are more practical to use because they hold 250MB or more information. When saving to these high-density disks, save your images at the highest resolution you possibly can. This way you'll have a high-quality image to use later as you wish.

It's helpful to create folders or subdirectories on the disk to help you catalog the images. If you've already created folders on your hard drive, you can simply drag and drop them into your archive media. If your media has a write-protected tab, set it to prevent you from accidentally writing over your archived images. Because these are also magnetic storage mediums, they are subject to the same problems.

Probably the most preferred way to archive images is to save them onto a CD. Two types of CDs are available for archiving. Again, a *CD readable* (CD-R) disc is a write-once media that cannot be erased. With a *CD read and write* (CD-RW) disc, you can update information if you decide to change an image and only want to save the revised image. As with any other storage media, store them in an area that is not prone to extreme temperatures, dust, or moisture. CDs are not as prone to damage, but you will want to protect them as they may be your only backup copy of your images.

Professional photographers store their images on CD-ROMs and some have even moved to DVDs as a larger storage facility for their raw files. It takes a lot of images to fill 4.7GB, and currently DVD is the best form of archiving. Even printing the images on paper isn't as permanent as storing them on disk. The inks and dyes will fade and the paper can change with the environment.

#188 How Photo Papers Differ

Many differences can be found in the various brands of photo paper, so get the best one you can afford. In general, the "off-the-shelf" inkjet paper from the likes of HP, Kodak, Canon, and Epson can pretty much be used with any of the printers from these manufacturers. However, if you're talking about the higher-quality, photo-type glossy and luster papers, these were carefully made to match the ink heads of the printer made by that particular manufacturer.

Some very good specialty papers work great with a number of inkjet printers. In your software program, select Print and notice the photo paper options it gives you. It will list brand names like Kodak, Fuji, and Epson, as well as "generic."

These no-name generic papers may not hold their colors as long, they may not be acid-free, and the inks in your printed image might not adhere correctly to the surface of the paper. Consequently, they are also cheaper than a manufacturer's paper. A package of generic paper may contain 200 sheets, and for the same price you might get 100 sheets of a brand name. The two kinds are different, however, and most of the time you will be able to see it.

You can get paper samples to try out in order to better help you decide which one is for you at the Red River Paper web site. It's located at www.redrivercatalog.com and is worth checking out.

Within the Kodak paper package, a page of instructions should be included on how to modify the printer settings (the information should also be available on the Kodak web site). If you follow the instructions very carefully, the Kodak paper will print well. If not, or if you use the default printer settings, you might get a smeared blob of ink. You must set the paper type and various other settings in order for the printer to work properly. Some find this to be a pain, which is why they usually stick with the printer manufacturer's paper.

#189 How to Use an Inkjet Printer

With the prices of printers falling, we've seen color inkjet printers for $30. The small print is that the ink cartridge costs more than the printer (if you can find it), but you still get your color photos.

You'd think that next to choosing a new computer, choosing a new printer would be a relatively straightforward process, but as anyone in the market for their first printer knows, just as many variables exist.

Inkjet printers, as the name implies, use various colored inks to get the image on the paper. The higher the quality of the print (the more dpi) the longer it's going to take to output. Advertisements for printers will tell you how many pages per minute the printer can produce for both black and white images and ones in color.

Unfortunately, they don't tell you that the resolution of the image will be small (sometimes 72 dpi) to get that amount of paper out in a short time. Instead, look for how long the photo resolution will take, if that's what you'll be using your printer for. The higher the dpi (such as 1220 × 2440), the sharper the photo, but the longer it will take to finish.

An inkjet printer will send the ink cartridge across the paper one line at a time by returning to the right again and printing another line. With an 8 × 10 image on photo paper, that's a lot of printing to do. For the best quality, which is what you normally want for a photograph, it could take over 20 minutes to print one image.

Another drawback to inkjet printers is that you must allow the ink to dry before you handle it. This can also take quite a bit of time. Some overzealous people will grab the print the second it exits the printer because they have been waiting so long, only to smear the ink with their fingers. They'll have no way to correct this and must start all over again. Inkjet printers are inexpensive, but for that low price you must spend time waiting for your printout.

The main decision points in choosing a printer can be broken down into five categories: type, quality, speed, consumables, and size. Each of these will be discussed in the following solutions.

#190 How to Use a Laser Printer

Are laser printers really worth the extra cost? The answer to that depends on the way you intend to use it. The images will look better, arrive in your hands faster than an inkjet, and may have a longer archival life.

Laser printers can be found at discount and photo stores. You insert your image on the scanner bed and your finished print is delivered via a laser print. One of the benefits of laser printers is that the image is dry as soon as you receive it because the toner has baked it on the photo paper, which is why it sometimes feels warm.

The individual colors will not smear and the dpi is usually greater on a laser printer than the best inkjet models. As mentioned in the other solutions, you'll need to determine how much you'll use your printer to justify the cost and expense of a laser model.

When we have clients that want a large number of 8 × 10 laser prints, we usually have a photo place do it to save the wear and tear on our equipment. No doubt about it, a color photo will take a lot of ink (or lasers?) to produce an image.

We once had an order for 100 laser print enlargements and the photo store we sent the work to had to change the toner cartridge three times during the printing. The laser printer looked like a color copier, but only 33 images per cartridge were printed. That justified charging the customer $9 per image; no toner cartridge costs that much, but it did save us from wearing out our printer.

#191 How to Choose a Type of Printer

Choosing a type of printer isn't difficult; you just need to determine what each type does. The basic printer categories are inkjet and laser, subdivided again into black and white and color, although it's getting difficult to find a black-and-white-only inkjet printer.

An inkjet does what it sounds like: It sprays ink, through very small jets, onto paper. Any kind of paper will work, but the ink will bleed through thin paper. For photographs, that type of paper won't cause any problems with bleed-throughs.

A laser printer uses a laser beam to "draw" an image onto a cylindrical drum, which then attracts black (or colored) toner ink onto its surface via an electrical charge. The drum then fuses the toner image onto the paper using heat and pressure. We'll go into more detail on laser printers in another solution.

Beyond the technology and quality, important differences exist between inkjets and lasers. These include the time to produce an image, longevity, and price.

#192 How to Choose the Quality of a Printer

Great differences exist in the quality of printers because they are not all created equal. Printer quality is a byproduct of resolution, which is measured in dpi. The more dpi, the finer the print and the better the resolution.

Despite what the ad copy may imply, a printer's real resolution is the product of both horizontal and vertical dpi. Many will print out fine in one direction (horizontal) yet print at a smaller, less dense resolution in the other (vertical) direction. Often you'll have to look at the technical spec sheets to see whether a 600-dpi printer has full 600 $\times$ 600 resolution or whether it's merely 600 $\times$ 300 dpi.

Laser printers usually have higher resolutions than inkjets, but since print quality is also largely dependent on the kind of paper you use, you'll find that many inkjets rival their laser counterparts in real-world usage.

#**193** How to Determine the Speed of a Printer

Printer speeds vary as greatly as the models that are available. You need to choose the fastest one your budget will allow, remembering the faster the printer, the higher the price.

Printer speeds are officially measured in *pages per minute* (PPM), but this rating can be highly misleading. For instance, "best speed" measurements are often taken from an economy mode setting that prints copy at a lower dpi than you would want for a formal business letter. Again, this is another example of why you'll want to really comb through the spec sheet.

Never believe what is written on the box. That's a best-world scenario. Instead, look at the instructions inside to see if this printer is really what you'll need for your photos.

The speed of laser printers and energy-efficient printers of all kinds can be significantly affected in a real-world setting by the fact that the machines go into standby mode when not in use, requiring them to wake up, initialize, and warm up the toner or ink. In other words, a really fast PPM rating is only useful if you regularly print out documents of 20 pages or more. It may not be worth the price if you print out smaller documents at erratic intervals throughout the day.

#**194** How Much Printer Memory Do You Need?

One of the factors that controls speed is the amount of memory your printer has. Much like a computer, memory controls how fast a processor can print an image.

The more *random access memory* (RAM) a printer has, the faster a large document will fully "spool" into the printer's memory and the sooner your computer will be freed from processing the print job. Waiting for your desktop to spool the print job may be more annoying than waiting for the actual pages to print out. Older inkjet printers could take several minutes before the job is processed and the clock is started for printing. In this case, you might be better off paying for more processing power at the cost of higher PPM speeds.

#**195** How Expensive Are Your Printer's Supplies?

Printer manufacturers don't often like to talk about how costly the supplies are, because once you purchase the unit, it becomes your problem.

Toner for laser printers is far more expensive than ink for inkjets, but toner lasts far longer. If you really do a lot of printing, and by that we mean printing long documents daily, a laser printer will cost less to maintain in the long run. Manufacturers will usually spell out how many pages you can expect to print from a given ink or toner cartridge. Take note of those numbers and use them as a comparison point.

Paper is as important a cost factor as ink and toner. To get really high-quality inkjet prints usually means you'll have to use special coated paper, which can cost three times as much as regular paper or more. Not all photo papers are created equal. Cheaper, nonbrand-name photo papers don't look as good as Kodak, Fuji, HP, and so on. A glossy paper will cost more and look different than a satin finish.

If a sales associate prints a demo page for you in a store, ask about the kind and cost of the photo paper. Request a printout on less expensive photo paper to get a feel for the difference.

Again, read the specs to see whether the manufacturer recommends a certain kind of paper to be used, and weigh those costs before making any decisions. Some printers even ask you what type of photo paper you're using to adjust the output to match.

We purchased 200 sheets of warehouse-brand, high-gloss photo paper. We got exactly what we paid for: not much.

#196 Which Size of Printer Best Suits Your Needs?

This may seem obvious, but like so many technical things it really isn't. How big is the printer? A printer is more than just its listed dimensions. Does it have a top-loading tray, as many of the "space-saving" inkjets do? If so, then don't plan to stuff it on a cramped shelf, because you'll need an additional 10 inches or so for the loaded paper to stand up.

How are the print trays configured? Will the tray stick over the edge of your desk, causing you to constantly bump into it throughout the day? Will you be able to easily take the trays out and refill the paper without having to perform an elaborate acrobatic move?

Exactly how do you load envelopes or special letterhead, and where is the power switch? Are all of these elements arrayed so that you'll be able to position the printer conveniently, or will you end up starting your day reaching around behind the machine, blindly searching for some inaccessible on-off switch?

#**197** How Many DPI Do I Need?

The age-old question of how many dpi are necessary depends on the final use of the image. The more dpi, the sharper and clearer the photograph, but it may be overkill with too much time and storage space being used to open and print the result.

Resolution refers to the sharpness and clarity of a picture, which is measured by the number of dpi. An image to be e-mailed or used on a web site could be as low as 72 dpi. A medium resolution is normally 200 to 300 dpi and can be used for viewing and smaller reproductions. A high resolution is generally 600 dpi or greater and used for larger-format printing, high-quality publications, and archival purposes.

When you archive your image at a higher resolution, you'll have everything covered. You can always use the image at a smaller size, but to be safe when archiving, go big. It takes up much more space, but you are allowing yourself more options.

#**198** How to Determine Quality Settings

Quality is a major concern when printing digital images. Depending on your printer, you may have a wide variety of options for how you can print an image.

Under *Properties* in your *Print* menu, you may be able to choose *Quick*, *Normal, Best*, or *Draft*, in addition to *Text*, *Text and Image*, *Photo*, and *Photo RPM*. With some printers, you can also adjust your *Resolution*, *Edge Smoothing*, and *Tone Saver*. With others, you may also be asked to select between *Photographic Images*, *Line Art*, or *Scanned Images*. If your intention is simply to print something only to have a hard copy on file, choose the fastest method, which will also use less toner or ink. The more dpi, the higher the resolution.

Unlike pixels, which can vary in size, dpi always represents a fixed number of dots per linear inch on the hard copy medium. A common resolution for laser printers is 600 dpi. This means 600 dots across and 600 down, so there are 360,000 dots per square inch. Obviously, the higher resolution you choose (dpi), the higher the quality of the finished image. Choosing the higher print quality usually reduces the speed of printing each page.

The term ppi or *pixels per inch* is most often used when scaling existing digital images to the required printing size. Although the terms ppi and dpi are relatively interchangeable, the term dpi is most appropriate when you're scaling media like film or scanned photos to a desired pixel resolution that is required for either printouts or monitor display.

#199 How to Use a Scanner

Before digital cameras came around, a scanner was the only way to get a photograph or image into the computer environment. Scanners can still be used with digital cameras; it's just another way to input visual information into your computer.

Scanners come in two forms and numerous sizes: combination and flatbed. Let's look at how the combination scanner works first.

The combination scanner is usually combined with a printer, copier, and fax machine. The image is inserted into the machine and the user must select what he or she wants to do: copy, fax, or scan. If scan is selected, the image is pulled into the unit and scanned internally. Upon completion, the artwork exits the unit and the scanned image appears on the computer's screen.

A flatbed scanner, as the name implies, is flat. The photo or artwork is placed on the flat glass surface. Its indicator marks allow you to line up your image, and most scanners have a glass top that is at least 11 × 14 in size. Larger scanners can accept bigger images, but the cost also escalates. The more dpi-capable your scanner, the higher the price. Purchase one that suits your needs.

Once the image is placed on the glass and the lid is closed, holding the artwork in place, the scanner can be activated. Before the scanning can begin, you must answer numerous questions about the image's characteristics, such as its size, whether it will be in color or black and white, and its quality (dpi). After these questions are answered, click the Scan icon and the scanning will begin.

A scanner will duplicate or capture anything that is on the glass surface, including dust, smudges, and debris. Make sure the surface has been cleaned carefully before you scan your artwork. Any imperfections on your artwork will be scanned also.

A light bar, much like that in a copying machine, will travel the length and width of the image, scanning it into a buffer or memory. When the image has been scanned, the light bar will travel back to its original spot. During this time, the image will be displayed on your computer screen and you can begin manipulating it or save it.

The Gettysburg National Military Park Museum is currently making 300,000 documents from the Civil War available online. Each of these

original, priceless, fragile documents it to be scanned and saved in a storage medium. One at a time, each document will be placed on a large, flatbed scanner by a technician wearing gloves. After two years, all this information will be available on the Internet, some of it never seen before because of the poor shape of the originals. This is just another way that digital imaging is preserving artifacts for future generations.

#199

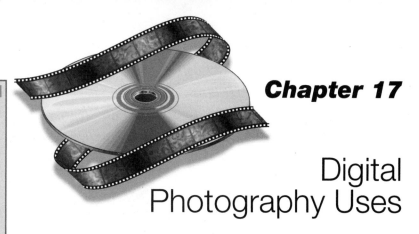

Chapter 17

Digital Photography Uses

#200 How to Photograph Animals in the Zoo

This can sometimes be a difficult place to shoot because the animals are confined, but it's a lot safer than trying to do it in the wild. The photographs we'll be showing you in this solution were all done in a zoo, but the trick is not letting the viewer know that.

Nothing is wrong with showing that the lion is in fact in a zoo. People probably won't think you shot it in your front yard or traveled to Africa last weekend. Our point is, don't go to great extremes to hide the fact that the animals are captive. Instead let the environment of the cage or setting work for you. Let's look at a few examples taken by a colleague, Larry Westberg.

Figure 17-1 shows a baby elephant on the move at the National Zoo in Washington, D.C. By using what you have learned in the action photography solution, pan with the elephant to blur the background. She was photographed in a zoo, but it's difficult to tell by the background.

Figure 17-2 shows an intimate moment with two gorillas. By using a telephoto lens and cropping out the background, the viewer feels as if he or she is sharing a private moment with them because the background isn't evident. Note the baby in her mother's arms.

Figure 17-3 illustrates what can happen by chance. With no trick photography or software enhancement, Larry captured these two leopards on a log with their tails entwined. It almost doesn't look real. Sometimes just waiting and being in the right place at the right time will get you a fantastic picture. Look for framing opportunities and take advantage of them.

Figure 17-4 shows a dolphin in the water. By zooming in extremely tight (with a 400mm lens) with a fast shutter speed

Figure 17-1

A baby elephant on the go.
(Photo by Larry Westberg)

#200

Figure 17-2

"Hey, can I lie
down too?"
(Photo by Larry
Westberg)

(1/500 of a second), Larry illustrates the calmness of the water and the texture of the dolphin's skin. By getting closer than most people would normally be able to, it makes the image that much more exciting.

Figure 17-5 looks more like a painting because of the high grain from shooting at 1600 ISO. Freezing the red wolf drinking, the graininess of the image enhances the fall foliage on the ground. A fast ISO allows a

Figure 17-3

"Is that your tail or mine?"
(Photo by Larry Westberg)

Figure 17-4

The kind of
dolphin that
doesn't play
football (Photo
by Larry
Westberg)

higher f-stop, keeping a deep depth of field. You still focus on the wolf without resorting to a blurred background.

Figure 17-6 is a majestic image of a Mexican wolf frozen in time. Surveying its kingdom at the zoo, Larry only needed to wait until he got the right pose from the lone predator. With no special lens or shutter tricks, patience was the key in getting this image.

Figure 17-5

"My tongue is stuck!" (Photo by Larry Westberg)

Sometimes great pictures just happen, but it also takes patience and talent behind the camera. The previous images were shot on a Canon EOS digital camera.

#201   How to Do Wedding Photography

Digital cameras have made wedding photography much easier, almost on the same level as wedding videos, where the only expense besides

Figure 17-6

"Who made that sound?"
(Photo by Larry Westberg)

the camera is a videotape (ours is the storage disk). So how can you shoot weddings with your digital camera and compete with the pros?

If you intend to do professional-quality work and shoot weddings, your style and camera need to mimic the professionals. Assist someone who shoots weddings to get the feel for the types of pictures and poses they create. Having a great camera doesn't make the professional; it's the talent behind the lens.

If you don't know any wedding photographers or if they won't let you tag along, offer to shoot someone's wedding with your digital camera as their wedding gift. Tell them it will be a learning experience for you, but they may want to use a professional if yours are going to be the only photographs taken that day. It is an important day and you don't want the entire burden resting on your shoulders.

When we were starting out, we asked to just take the informal portraits of the couple before the wedding. This way you have no pressure on you, the big day hasn't arrived, and you are in a relaxed setting.

Great books have been written on how to shoot weddings with excellent poses, shots, and lighting, so we'll leave that part of the discussion to those books, but we'll discuss how to use your digital camera to get some great shots. We've made the transition from 35mm photos to medium format to high-quality digital that rivals 120mm film.

A point and shoot digital camera may not be good enough to shoot a wedding. You need as many megapixels as you can afford in order to compete with high-end 35mm and 120mm shots. We typically use Nikon's D100, Fuji's SR2 (Nikon lenses fit both), or a Canon D60, all rated with at least six megapixels. The only other items are lots of storage (300 to 600 images) and extra lenses.

Obviously, the best thing about digital is being able to preview the image immediately to make sure you got the shot you want. We do most of this during the actual ceremony when we are taking pictures because this cannot be repeated. We usually shoot without a flash to avoid disturbing anyone to make sure we have enough light.

When shooting formal portraits, we won't check the *liquid crystal display* (LCD) after every shot, only if we apply some special effects filter to make sure it's what we're after. The same is true with the family images and candids at the reception. You need to devise a plan of attack to know exactly what type of photos you're after and how to get them in the shortest amount of time. The photographer naturally sets the pace of the day and if he or she gets behind schedule, the entire wedding is running late.

Let's take a look at a typical day in the life of a wedding photographer, this time equipped with a digital still camera. We arrive at the bride's house to show her getting ready. We often shoot these images in black and white to show the transition from single black-and-white life to married color (just like real-life marriages will be colorful). At least

Figure 17-7

The bride in black and white

50 images are shot of this progress, including the bride wearing her dress. Figure 17-7 shows the bride filtered with soft daylight.

At the church the men are shot clowning around with semiposed shots. This helps the guys relax and we usually get some great shots. The bride and her parents and family are also done before the service. We usually show the bride and her parents how great she looks in her gown via the LCD screen. This helps the bride relax, it shows you're a professional, and you get to see if your camera still works.

Don't make a habit of showing people your great shots. Just do that with a few early on to help put everyone at ease. During the ceremony, don't use a flash, but change your ISO rating to get clear, well-exposed shots without the distracting flash of light. Don't be afraid to change your ISO often as your environment changes.

The receiving line after the service, the family shots, and the bird seed or rice shots can be taken in quick order. Just check occasionally to make sure you have properly exposed images and save your battery. The biggest expense of most photographers is the cost of the film stock, processing, and printing. Your cost is now just the printing. Try and get some high shutter speed shots of the rice or bird seed in midair.

Sometimes informal shots are taken at a park or convenient location, as well as images in the limo on the way. These will be shots that no one else ever gets because you are the only photographer present.

At the reception, get the best shots you can because this is the couple's time to relax and unwind. Everyone has cameras, disposable units may be on each table, and people will start to get silly.

The bride and groom won't want many posed shots unless they call you over to get a shot of them hugging Uncle Milfred. Be at their beck and call, and the lights will dim as the alcohol flows and the night progresses, so be ready for that.

Before the night is over, set up a time that the couple can review the images, usually soon after the honeymoon. Everyone else will be showing them their photos right after the wedding, and photographers that take six months or longer to complete an album are losing out. You have the immediacy of digital (even faster than one-hour photos), so use that to your advantage and strike while the iron is hot.

The couple, fresh from their honeymoon, will want to consult others before the final album is put together, but at least give them images to help make their decision. Once their choices have been made, touch up any images before putting them in the album. Only fine-tune the images slightly after they see them and make any grand changes beforehand. They may like some little nuance in an image and you may destroy that in a software program. The particulars on how you handle everything is up to you. Just use your digital camera to its fullest.

#202 How to Shoot for Humor

Bringing a smile to someone's face with your digital images is just another way you can make your statement without the use of words. Humorous images don't need captions and the viewer may come up with a better one than you. We decided to end this book on a humorour note.

These humorous photographs must tell the story visually, whether it's someone or something in unusual surroundings; strange framing, lighting, or angles; something that is just funny to look at; or misplaced

Figure 17-8

You tell us what this means.

or mismatched images. We'll give you four examples and discuss why each is funny in its own right.

The first image, Figure 17-8, shows what a robin did on her own when building a nest. The humor in this image is just recording something that happened naturally but that most may not see unless someone happens upon it like we did. Needing something to add to her nest, a label from a Martha Stewart towel added nicely to her new home for raising young ones. This just goes to prove that Martha Stewart's touch is everywhere, even in a bird's nest.

Of course, you could stage something like this, but the real humor is not artificial. This would be an example of something plain in different or unusual surroundings.

Figure 17-9 is something that is unusual or funny to look at. The image is of an actual home that happens to be shaped like a shoe. The interior is normal, but the concrete outside is what makes the picture funny. This image doesn't take any unusual planning to make it humorous. Just take an picture of it as it exists.

The next example is of something that is humorous because of the angle at which you shot it. Sometimes getting really close or very low will make something look quite strange. An example of this would be someone standing close to the camera on one side of the shot with a

Figure 17-9

The real big shew (sic)

tall building or object on the other side of the shot and far in the background. It's almost as if the person and the building are the same size (although they are far apart and of completely different sizes). The distance perspective is off and it makes an appealing image.

Science fiction films use this principle. For example, a model spaceship can be filmed at just a few inches from the camera, framed at one side of the shot, while people are seen (from a great distance) walking away from the ship on the other side of the shot. The end result is that it appears as if the people have exited the spaceship; you have manipulated the viewer's perspective.

Another good example of an unusual shot is in Figure 17-10. The young man is pouring milk, but the milk stream is angled, barely hitting the glass. This is an old trick that Ernie Kovacks did on his TV show to create a strange visual effect. The set and camera are tilted at the exact same angle while the person must sit perfectly straight in relation to that angle. In our case, the camera, actor, and set were tilted 40 degrees to the left. When he poured the milk sitting like that, gravity made it flow downward and at an angle.

The last image, Figure 17-11, illustrates another example of something that is funny to look at. The car is something out of the late 1950s and brings back memories of the days when sheriffs' vehicles looked

Figure 17-10

Got milk?

Figure 17-11

Mayberry,
where are you?

#202

like this. With someone from the present standing next to something in the past, the result is humorous.

Try to find or capture images like these when using your digital camera and you can create a few smiles of your own.

Glossary

What Are Some Digital Terms You Should Know?

This glossary is a list of the terms used in digital photography that you should be aware of. Study them carefully because there won't be a test in the morning.

Aperture priority   In this mode, you adjust the aperture (the lens opening) and the camera adjusts the shutter speed for the correct exposure.

Archive   A file storage on a floppy disk, CD, or tape for future reference.

Backlight   Light falling behind your subject as opposed to on the subject.

Bitmap   An arrangement of pixels made up of binary numbers (1's and 0's) in rows and columns to form a basic image.

Bracketing   Taking several pictures from the same location of the same subject with variations of aperture and shutter speed to get the best overall exposure.

Burn   To make a part of an image darker using a photo-editing tool such as the Photoshop toning tool Burn Mode.

Cache   An area of memory used for saving information that can be easily accessed, more so than a disk or CD.

Cast   Normally, an undesired color affecting your desired color.

CCD raw format   The uninterpolated data collected directly from the image sensor before processing.

Charge-coupled device (CCD)   An image sensor that reads the charges built up on the sensor's photo sites a row at a time and storing them in a file. This is how a digital camera records an image.

Clone   Using the Rubber Stamp tool, copy pixels from one part of an image to another. An exact duplicate of something in every way.

Color balance   The overall accuracy with which the colors in a photograph match or are capable of matching those in the original scene.

Color correction   To improve the accuracy of the colors in your image.

Compact flash   A removable memory storage device.

Compression   A reduction in the size of a file. Some forms of compression preserve all the detail in the original, while others (such as JPEG) can reduce the quality of the image.

Contrast   The range of tones between the darkest and lightest shades within an image.

Crop   To alter or trim an image to contain only what you want to show.

Depth of field   The zone of sharpness, which will vary depending on your aperture and subject distance. The larger the aperture (lens opening), the smaller the zone of sharpness will be.

Dodge   Blocking part of an image as it's being exposed, which will result in lightening its tones.

Dots per inch (dpi)   The resolution of an image through the number of pixels or printer dots per inch.

Export   Transferring images or text using the Export functions option.

File format   A method in which an application stores information onto a disk.

Filter   A feature through an image editor that changes pixels in an image to produce unique special effects.

Flash card reader   An accessory that attaches to your computer by cable. You insert a flash memory card into the reader to transfer files.

Flash memory   A form of memory using chips instead of magnetic media. The data in the device isn't lost when the power is turned off.

Flash memory card   A card containing chips that store images.

FlashPix An image format that contains a number of resolutions, each of which is broken into tiles that can be edited and displayed independently.

Flash, slave A flash that fires when it senses the light from another flash unit.

Focal length The distance from the optical center of the lens to the image sensor when the lens is focused on infinity. The focal length is usually expressed in millimeters (mm) and determines the angle of view (how much of the scene can be included in the picture) as well as the size of the objects in the image. The longer the focal length, the narrower the angle of view and the more that objects are magnified.

f-stop The size of the lens opening. The larger f-stop numbers admit less light and the smaller f-stop numbers admit more light.

Gamma A numerical way of representing the contrast of an image's midtones.

Gaussian blur filter This filter quickly blurs a selection by an adjustable amount. *Gaussian* refers to the bell-shaped curve that is generated when Adobe Photoshop applies a weighted average to the pixels, adds low-frequency detail, and can produce a hazy effect.

GIF An image file format designed for displaying line art on the Web.

Highlight The brightest values in a continuous tone image.

Hot shoe A clip on the top of the camera that attaches to a flash unit and provides an electrical link to synchronize the flash with the camera shutter.

ISO (International Standards Organization) A number rating indicating the relative sensitivity to light of an image sensor or photographic film. Faster film (with a higher ISO) is more sensitive to light and requires less exposure than slower film.

JPEG (Joint Photographic Expert Group) JPEG compression economizes on the way data is stored. It identifies and discards extra data that is not essential to the display of the image.

Lasso A tool that allows you to make a selection by drawing a free-hand outline around an area.

LCD (Liquid Display Crystal)　Used to view the actual image seen through your camera's lens.

Magic Wand　An image editor tool that allows you to select portions of an image based on the color similarities of adjacent pixels.

Marquee　A tool that lets you select rectangular or elliptical areas by dragging around in a certain area of the image.

Memory stick　A flash memory storage device developed by Sony.

Noise　Random pixels added to an image to increase a graininess effect.

PC card　A card that plugs into a slot in a notebook or handheld computer. In the case of cameras, it is usually a storage device. PC cards were originally called PCMCIA cards.

Pixel　A picture element of a screen image.

Plug-in　An image editor filter.

Polarizing filter　This can enhance the contrast between clouds and a blue sky, for example, or reduce the glare from shiny objects such as chrome or glass.

Resolution　An indication of the sharpness of images on a printout or the display screen. It is based on the number and density of the pixels used. The more pixels used in an image, the more detail can be seen and the higher the image's resolution.

Rubber Stamp　This takes a sample of part of an image and places an exact copy (or clone) of that sample elsewhere in the same image or in another image.

SCSI port　A port that's faster than the serial and parallel ports, but slower and harder to configure than the newer USB port. Also known as the Small Computer System Interface.

Serial port　A very slow port on the computer used mainly by modems. Many digital cameras come equipped with cable to download images through this port, but it's slow! Both parallel and USB ports are faster connections.

Sharpening　Increasing the apparent sharpness of an image by increasing the contrast between adjacent pixels that form an edge.

Shutter priority   In this mode, you can set the shutter speed and the camera will adjust the aperture to provide the correct exposure.

SmartMedia   A type of removable memory storage device.

Sony Memory Stick   A type of removable memory storage device from Sony usually with a smaller amount of storage.

Unsharp masking   The process of increasing the contrast between adjacent pixels in an image, resulting in increased sharpness.

USB (Universal Serial Bus)   An interface used to connect digital cameras to a computer.

Index

About the Author

George H. Wallace has been a professional photographer for more than 20 years. A resident of Mechanicsburg, PA, he was previously the Manager of Photographic and Imaging Services for EXCEL Productions, Inc. and Supervisor of Corporate Photography for AMP, Incorporated.

Chuck Gloman is an independent producer, videographer, director, and film media editor. He has 23 years of experience in video, from commercial production to corporate training. He writes regularly for the publications *Videography*, *Mix*, and *Government Video*. He is the author of *No Budget Digital Filmmaking* and *303 Digital Filmmaking Solutioins*, also published by McGraw-Hill.